TOTAL QUALITY MANAGEMENT IN ACTION

Howard S. Gitlow

Shelly J. Gitlow

PTR Prentice Hall
Englewood Cliffs, New Jersey 07632

Library of Congress Cataloging-in-Publication Data

Editorial/Production Supervision: Lisa Iarkowski
Interior Design: Dit Mosco and Lisa Iarkowski
Acquisitions Editor: Mike Hays
Manufacturing Manager: Alexis R. Heydt
Cover Photo: Lou Odor Photography
Jacket Design: Lundgren Graphics

© 1994 PTR Prentice Hall
Prentice-Hall, Inc.
A Paramount Communications Company
Englewood Cliffs, NJ 07632

The publisher offers discounts on this book when ordered in bulk quantities.
For more information, contact:

Corporate Sales Department
PTR Prentice Hall
113 Sylvan Avenue
Englewood Cliffs, NJ 07632
Phone: 201-592-2863
FAX: 201-592-2249.

Printed in the United States of America

10 9 8 7 6 5 4 3 2 1

ISBN 0-13-138603-4

90000

9 780131 386037

Prentice-Hall International (UK) Limited, London
Prentice-Hall of Australia Pty. Limited, Sydney
Prentice-Hall of Canada, Inc., Toronto
Prentice-Hall Hispanoamericana S.A., Mexico
Prentice-Hall of India Private Limited, New Delhi
Prentice-Hall of Japan, Inc., Tokyo
Simon & Schuster Asia Pte. Ltd., Singapore
Editora Prentice-Hall do Brasil, Ltd., Rio de Janeiro

To our daughter Ali

We wish you smooth sailing on your "River of Dreams."

C ontents

CONTENTS

Preface

Do you remember your first kiss? You probably do. You probably also remember the prelude to that kiss: reading, watching movies, practicing on your hand, and endless discussions about the impending event with your equally inexperienced friends. By the time you actually puckered up, you knew everything there was to know about the "theory of kissing." You just didn't know exactly how to translate that theory into practice. We assume you made that jump over the chasm between theory and practice, even if it was purely by force of hormonal propulsion.

Total Quality Management is coming of age in the United States. It's time to put theory into practice. Since the early 1980s, interested people have read books and journals, attended seminars and training sessions, and watched films and videos in an earnest attempt to learn about TQM. Their education has been frustrating because although they embrace the theory, it is difficult for them to apply it in their organizations. What is needed is an integrated approach that explains the theory and how to put it into practice using a step-by-step method.

Total Quality Management in Action is a model of TQM that combines the theoretical base of Dr. W. Edwards Deming and the practical techniques of the Japanese administrative systems into a useful application for those people who have been wondering, "How do we get started and actually 'do' quality?" It is a fork-shaped model that includes the handle of the fork (Management's Commitment to Transformation) and four prongs (Management's Intellectual and Emotional Education, Daily Management, Cross-Functional Management, and Policy Management). To facilitate understanding, numerous organizational, personal, and familial examples are provided.

P REFACE

Management's Commitment to Transformation, the handle of the fork, is clearly the most essential element of any TQM undertaking. American management has to be ready to digest the theory of TQM and put it into practice. This has not been an easy meal to swallow, and they are certainly not the only group that is reluctant to change. For example, surgeons were very hesitant to go from theory to practice. It was postulated that the washing of hands before surgery could prevent infection; however, it took surgeons 200 years before they put theory into practice and scrubbed up before operating. It is our sincere hope that managers will be more open-minded and enthusiastic about transformation.

Dr. Deming passed away on December 20, 1993. His dream was "to save America from committing suicide." His philosophy of management will endure. He never wavered in his mission to transform American management. For those of us who were lucky enough to have been touched by Dr. Deming, a goal remains. We have to maintain a focused sense of purpose, disseminating his theories, building on them, and working with people in all types of organizations to make "joy in work" a part of everyone's life. We offer *Total Quality Management in Action* as a monument to Dr. Deming's perseverance, tenacity, and unfaltering dedication to his mission.

A Model for Total Quality Management

D r. Deming's Theory of Management

In 1980, Dr. Deming developed 14 interrelated points for management. Together, they provide a road map for Western leaders who want to transform their organizations.[1] These points are as follows:

---

1. The 14 points are discussed in Deming, W.E., *Out of the Crisis* (1986), MIT Center for Advanced Engineering Study (Cambridge, MA) and Gitlow and Gitlow *The Deming Guide to Quality and Competitive Position*, (1987), Prentice-Hall (Englewood Cliffs, NJ).

Purpose of this Chapter

The purpose of this chapter is to provide an overview of the "Model for Total Quality Management" presented in this book. The model combines Dr. W. Edwards Deming's theory of management and Japanese Total Quality Control into an integrated and internally consistent plan for the transformation of an organization.

A Model for the Transformation of an Organization

1. Create constancy of purpose toward improvement of product and service, with the aim to become competitive and to stay in business and to provide jobs.

2. Adopt the new philosophy. We are in a new economic age. Western management must awaken to the challenge, must learn their responsibilities, and take on leadership for change.

3. Cease dependence on inspection to achieve quality. Eliminate the need for inspection on a mass basis by building quality into the product in the first place.

4. End the practice of awarding business on the basis of price tag. Instead, minimize total cost. Move toward a single supplier for any one item, with a long-term relationship of loyalty and trust.

5. Improve constantly and forever the system of production and service, to improve quality and productivity and thus constantly decrease costs.

6. Institute training on the job.

7. Institute leadership. The aim of leadership should be to help people and machines and gadgets to do a better job. Leadership of management is in need of overhaul, as well as leadership of production workers.

8. Drive out fear, so that everyone may work effectively for the company.

9. Break down barriers between departments. People in research, design, sales, and production must work as a team to foresee problems in production and in use

that may be encountered with the product or service.

10. Eliminate slogans, exhortations, and targets for the work force that ask for zero defects and new levels of productivity.

11. Eliminate work standards (quotas) on the factory floor. Substitute leadership. Eliminate management by objective. Eliminate management by numbers and numerical goals. Substitute leadership.

12. Remove barriers that rob the hourly worker of his right to pride of workmanship. The responsibility of supervisors must be changed from stressing sheer numbers to quality. Remove barriers that rob people in management and engineering of their right to pride of workmanship. This means, *inter alia*, abolishment of the annual merit rating and management by objective.

13. Encourage education and self-improvement for everyone.

14. Take action to accomplish the transformation.

Then in 1989, Dr. Deming presented the underlying theory of quality management, "The System of Profound Knowledge."[2] The reader is directed to the source in footnote two for an in-depth discussion of The System of Profound Knowledge. A brief discussion of the System of Pro-

2. The System of Profound Knowledge was first distributed in 1989 as the hard copy of a presentation Dr. Deming made in Japan. In 1993 it was published in Deming, W.E., *The New Economics: For Industry, Government, Education*, MIT Center for Advanced Engineering Study (Cambridge, MA), 1993.

found Knowledge is presented in the appendix at the end of this chapter.

System of Profound Knowledge

The purpose of the System of Profound Knowledge is to transform Western leaders so that they will:

1. improve and innovate the system of interdependent stakeholders of an organization over the long term to allow all people to experience joy in their work and pride in the outcome. Stakeholders include employees, customers, suppliers, stockholders, the community, and competitors.

2. optimize the system of interdependent stakeholders of an organization over the long term so that everybody wins.

3. improve and innovate the condition of society. Society includes local, regional, national, and international systems; for example, the entire educational system (public and private schools; primary and secondary schools and universities), the environment, public health, and the economic and social well-being of communities and countries.

Paradigm Shifts A paradigm is a way of looking at the world. That way determines how an individual processes information and behaves. Dr. Deming's System of Profound Knowledge is an example of a new paradigm of management.

Consider the following paradigm of pronunciation. Say the word "ghoti" out loud. Based on the traditional paradigm of pronunciation, you probably said "goaty, gotty or hotty." There is another way to pronounce the word, based on a different paradigm of pronunciation. Pronounce the "gh" as in trough (f), the "o" as in women (i), and the "ti" as in nation (sh). Using the new paradigm, "ghoti" is pronounced "fish."

Accepting paradigm shifts is very difficult. If you overcome your need to rely on traditional models and change your paradigm of pronunciation, you will incorporate the new pronunciation into your daily speech. There will be serious consequences. People will not understand you. Some might even think you've lost your mind. You will be a lone soul, unless you can convince others to accept the new paradigm.

This is exactly what happens to those leaders who try to embrace the new paradigms for management, as described by Dr. Deming. Changing paradigms is a monumental task because people cling to them for a sense of security.

Existing Paradigms

In the Western world, leaders use paradigms, often without realizing that they are getting in the way of successful management. Some examples of existing paradigms are:

1. Rewards and punishments bring out the best in people.

2. Focusing on results yields improvement of results.

3. Crisis intervention will improve an organization in the long term.

4. Effective decisions can be made using "gut feel."

5

5. Rational decisions can be made using only visible figures.

6. Quality and quantity cannot be achieved together.

7. Your most important customer is your superior.

8. Management's function is to construct, execute, and control plans.

9. Competition is superior to cooperation, and winners and losers are necessary in any interaction.

Western leaders who manage in the context of the above paradigms are unable to survive in the new economic order. They don't know how to manage their organizations based on the new paradigms required for success in today's marketplace. Such leaders need a perspective from which they can understand and integrate the new paradigms of management.

New Paradigms   The System of Profound Knowledge explains four paradigm shifts that are necessary for organizational success in the 21st century. They are very different from traditional corporate paradigms. They are:

Paradigm 1

Manage to create a win-win environment, not a win-lose environment. The focus of a win-win environment is optimization of all stakeholders in the organization's system of interdependent stakeholders.

An example of the need to create a win-win environment occurs frequently in the management of family systems. The Carroll family is made up of four interdependent stakeholders:

6

mother, Joan, father, Paul, twelve-year-old Gary, and eight-year-old Lucy. They have a problem.

In spite of Paul and Joan's desire to add a bathroom to their home, they have been unable to afford the renovation. They all share one bathroom and have to leave the house at approximately the same time in the morning. Joan and Paul drive Lucy to school on their way to work. Gary takes the school bus.

Paul and Joan receive a letter from Gary's school. He has been late to school 14 times in the past month. If it continues, he will have to serve detention each day he is late. Joan's initial reaction is to blame Gary and punish him (the old paradigm). Paul, however, has just attended a Deming seminar on the System of Profound Knowledge and has some other ideas.

He realizes that Gary gets up on time and does all his morning tasks in a timely manner. He also realizes that Gary is always the last one to use the bathroom because he and Joan have to get to work on time. Lucy goes before Gary because she has to leave with the parents. He explains to Joan that Gary is being penalized while everyone else is meeting his or her goal of getting to work or school on time. They decide to change the system so that everyone wins.

Paul and Joan hold a family meeting with Gary and Lucy in which they discuss what can be done to change the system so that they all can meet their goals. They come up with a short-term solution and a long-term plan.

7

Paul will get up 15 minutes earlier, so that he can use the bathroom before anyone else is up. Joan and Lucy will have their allotted time, leaving Gary with 15 minutes before he has to leave. Paul doesn't mind getting up earlier, and Joan and Lucy agree to keep track of their time. Gary appreciates the familial support and will make it to school on time. They agree to meet in a week and discuss how the system is working.

For the long term, Joan and Paul set up a savings plan so that they will have the funds to renovate the bathroom as soon as possible. The whole family suggests ways that they are willing to cut back in other areas to facilitate the funding of the bathroom renovation. These managers have created a win-win environment with their willingness to accept the new paradigm. They no longer look to punish an individual, but seek to change the system for the optimization of all members.

Paradigm 2

Manage to create intrinsic motivation, not extrinsic motivation. Intrinsic motivation is the individual's desire to do something for the sheer joy of it. Extrinsic motivation is the individual's desire to do something to gain rewards or to avoid punishments.

Intrinsic motivation releases human energy, which can be focused into improvement and innovation of the system of interdependent stakeholders. Extrinsic motivation restricts the release of energy from intrinsic motivation by judging, policing, and destroying the individual.

"READ ON" is a very popular educational program. It is sponsored by elementary schools, and its purpose is to encourage children to read. At first glance, this sounds like a constructive undertaking. However, it destroys intrinsic motivation by making children want to read for an extrinsic reward, as opposed to reading for the joy of it.

Each child fills out a list of the books he or she has read, along with the number of pages. The children are rewarded with certificates when they reach certain numbers of books or pages. Parents are encouraged to donate money to the school, based on the amount that a child or class has read. There is no consideration of whether the child actually read the book, understood it, or liked it. In fact, this system may cause some children to lie about the number of books being read.

The focus is on creating the list and getting the rewards. For children who already like to read, having to make the list is unnecessary. They already have the intrinsic motivation to read. And for those children who haven't acquired a taste for reading, making a list and getting extrinsic rewards won't make them want to read for the sake of reading. Teaching them how to read and guiding them to reading material that they enjoy will make them avid readers

Paradigm 3

Manage with a long-term process and results orientation, not with a short-term results-only orientation. A long-term process and results orientation promotes improvement and innovation of organizational processes. Highly capable processes facilitate prediction of the future and, consequently, a higher likelihood of achieving the organizational mission.

A restaurant manager, George, complains that he can't find competent servers. He is in a never-ending cycle of personnel turnover because servers break too many dishes.

George manages with a short-term results orientation. He wants each wait person to serve at least 30 meals per shift. This creates enormous pressure to work fast. The floor in the restaurant is tiled and very slippery. Sometimes, when a server scurries to bring a tray, he or she slips and drops the tray, breaking dishes and glassware.

In an effort to cut down the breakage, George makes the servers pay for the broken items. If George decides that too many pieces have been destroyed in a particular evening, he fires the responsible party. Servers often quit because they are frustrated by the breakage policy. George is on a treadmill and blames the personnel for the problem.

If George managed with a long-term process and results orientation, he would be able to get off the treadmill. He would understand that he has a "breakage process" that is in control, and that the only way to change it is to alter the process, not get rid of the workers.

If George managed with a long-term process and results orientation, he would talk to the servers. They would tell him that the reason they break things is that the floor is too slippery, and they are under too much pressure to work fast. He would know that as a manager, it is his responsibility to improve the "breakage system" and create an environment in which the servers can work toward achieving the restaurant's mission.

Paradigm 4

Manage to promote cooperation, not competition. In a cooperative environment, everybody wins. The customer wins products and services he can brag about and rejects commonly accepted levels of defects, rework, shoddy workmanship, and poor service. The firm wins returns for investors and secure jobs for employees. Suppliers win long-term customers for their products. The community wins an excellent corporate citizen.

In a competitive environment, most people lose. The costs resulting from competition are unknown and unknowable, but they are huge. Competition causes individuals, or departments, to optimize their own efforts at the expense of other stakeholders. This form of optimization seriously erodes the performance of the system of interdependent stakeholders.

The field of medical research provides an example of the need to promote cooperation as opposed to competition. Currently, hospitals, universities, and practitioners throughout the world compete for resources and recognition in the various areas of medical research. This creates a situation in which everyone loses.

Patients (customers) are shortchanged because they are deprived of the benefits that sharing resources and information would yield, including more timely and effective cures for diseases.

Researchers (employees) lose because they are under pressure to produce results to secure funding over other researchers and are deprived of a creative exchange of ideas to stimulate their studies.

Hospitals and universities (firms) lose because they are never sure of their funding and cannot adequately plan for the long term.

The community suffers great financial, physical, and emotional losses because of the lack of coordination in medical research.

The AIDS crisis necessitates a more cooperative approach to research. The medical community has taken a step in the right direction with a yearly international symposium where researchers and clinicians meet to share information. A cooperative environment such as this optimizes the system of interdependent stakeholders.

Patients get access to new treatments in a more timely fashion. Researchers get stimulation from each other, and hospitals and universities improve their research processes. The community is greatly improved by attending to a medical crisis in a more organized, coordinated effort.

It is unfortunate that a crisis situation has to exist before such cooperative efforts are undertaken. All community problems deserve this type of focused interchange of ideas and information.

**Applying
the System
of Profound
Knowledge**

Each leader's concept of the new practice of management is based on the System of Profound Knowledge. However, even with that common theoretical base, leaders in an organization will have different interpretations of how they should practice management. Top management's task is to reduce individual-to-individual variation in respect to understanding the System of Profound Knowledge through education, training, and mentoring.

Since organizations are unique, with their own nuances and idiosyncrasies, managers in one organization cannot rely on the experiences of managers in other organizations to focus their transformation efforts. The conditions that led to the experiences of the managers in one organization may not exist for the managers of the other organization.

The experiences of managers in one organization can stimulate the development of theories for improvement and innovation for managers of another organization. However, the leadership of each organization should develop its own model to operationalize the System of Profound Knowledge and the 14 points, integrating the "personality" of the organization.

Japanese Total Quality Control

After World War II, the economy of Japan was decimated. The leadership of Japan faced terrible economic and social crises. In the early 1950s, the Japanese Union of Scientists and Engineers

(JUSE) invited Dr. Deming to speak to Japan's leading industrialists. At the time, he was the only person who offered any hope toward the resolution of Japan's problems.

Despite their reservations, Dr. Deming convinced the Japanese industrialists that by instituting his ideas, their quality could become the best in the world. Dr. Deming taught the Japanese: the value of the Plan-Do-Study-Act (PDSA) cycle, the managerial significance of the distinction between special and system causes of variation, the value of statistical methods on the factory floor, that quality concepts are equally applicable in manufacturing and non-manufacturing environments, and to view an organization as a system (an interdependent system of stakeholders). The industrialists took Dr. Deming's teachings to heart and Japanese quality, productivity, and competitive position were improved and strengthened tremendously.

It is interesting to note that Dr. Deming's 14 points did not appear until 1980. What were the Japanese doing in respect to quality management between 1950 and 1980? The answer is that they[3] had taken the teachings of Deming and others and created their own school of thought on quality management, Japanese Total Quality Control (TQC).

---

3. In 1949, JUSE formed the famous QC Research Group. Its members included Dr. Shigeru Mizuno, Dr. Kaoru Ishikawa, Mr. Masao Goto, Mr. Hidehiko Higashi, Dr. Tetsuichi Asaka, Dr. Masao Kogure, Mr. Shin Miura, and Mr. Eizo Watanabe.

Japanese TQC is empirically based on the experiences of what works in Japanese companies. It is unlike Dr. Deming's theory of management, which is theoretically based. Furthermore, Japanese TQC has highly developed administrative systems by which organizational leaders can practice quality management. This is in contrast to Dr. Deming's theory of management, in which the leadership of each organization must develop its own administrative systems for quality management.

Japanese quality experts, with guidance from Dr. Joseph Juran and others, gave the world a great gift in the administrative systems of TQC. Administrative systems include education, training, and self-improvement; daily management; cross-functional management; and policy management. These systems are described in the following section.

A Model for Quality Management

Background

Top management, including the Board of Directors, initiates and leads quality management efforts. One of the first tasks for top management is to learn about the various theories, models, and techniques in the field. Then top management formulates a quality management model suited to the nuances of its organization. Quality management models will differ from organization to organization.

The Model

This book presents one possible model of quality management. Its theoretical base is Dr. Deming's System of Profound Knowledge, and its practical base is the administrative systems of Japanese TQC. The administrative systems of Japanese TQC have been modified to be in harmony with the System of Profound Knowledge and the 14 points. This model is presented to stimulate the thinking of top managers when they develop a quality management model for their organization. It represents an "ideal" for promoting quality management, which must be continuously pursued, and improved, by the leadership of an organization.

The model presents a possible sequencing of activities which could be used to transform an organization (see Figure 1.1).

A Model for the Transformation of an Organization

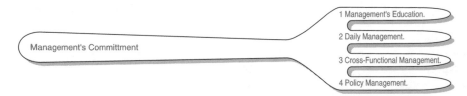

Figure 1.1

The model is shaped like a fork with a handle and four prongs. The handle is "management's commitment to transformation." The first prong is "management's intellectual and emotional education." The second prong is "daily management." The third prong is "cross-functional management," and the fourth prong is "policy management." Each part of the fork is described below.

The fork analogy is used because quality management is an implement of nourishment for an organization. It feeds an organization, so its people have the energy to transform and pursue their goal of never-ending improvement.

The Handle: Management's Commitment to Transformation

Management's commitment to transform an organization is represented by the handle of the fork. The handle binds the prongs and directs the action of the system. Without the handle, there is no fork. This is the case with quality management. Top management generates and directs the energy necessary to transform an organization. Top managers will expend this energy if they are confronted with a crisis or if they have a vision that they want to pursue.[4]

An example of management's commitment to transformation can be seen in the following situation. The Kelly family has experienced a crisis. Mr. Kelly lost his job and is unable to find a new one. Mr.and Mrs. Kelly have to direct the family to transform its fiscal policies so that it can survive on one salary, instead of two. Their commitment to change comes from the impact of a crisis. On the other hand, the Lang family has a vision. Mr. and Mrs. Lang want to save money so that their children can attend college. They realize that saving at their current rate is not enough.

---

4. Kano, Noriaki, "A Perspective on Quality Activities in American Firms," *California Management Review,* Spring 1993, pp. 14-15. See Quality Sweating Theory.

They lead the family in changing its fiscal policies so that the focus is on saving more money. Their commitment to transformation comes from a long-term vision to provide the resources for the children's education.

Top management retains outside counsel to obtain expertise in the System of Profound Knowledge and to help management recognize its own strengths and weaknesses. The window of opportunity for the transformation opens. The outside expert assists top management in developing a plan for the transformation of the organization.

The top management then forms an Executive Committee (EC) which consists of all policy makers in the organization. The objective of the EC is to carry out the plan for transformation. This is accomplished by educating all members of the EC, as well as the members of the Board of Directors and stockholders (to the extent possible). The EC also develops a plan to communicate transformation activities to all relevant stakeholders.

Once the above phase of education and training is complete, the window of opportunity for transformation begins to close, *unless* the members of the EC exhibit concrete signs of transformation to relevant stakeholders. These signs include entering a period of education and self-improvement (prong one), performing daily management (prong two), conducting cross-functional management (prong three), and performing policy management (prong four).

Prong One: Management's Intellectual and Emotional Education

Prong one symbolizes the education of top managers. Studying the System of Profound Knowledge, the 14 points, and a transformation model is necessary to understand the theoretical and practical underpinnings of the new management. It will also provide insight to help cope with the upheaval that results from the transformation.

For example, the top management of an organization has made a commitment to transform their company through quality management. They hire a consultant to help them study the necessary theoretical information and integrate it into a model specific to their organization. The consultant also gives them feedback on their treatment of employees and the dynamics of how they interact with each other.

Mr. Harris, the CEO, is told that he is autocratic and uncompromising with employees; he needs to modify his behavior to be able to transform the organization. Ms. Gardner, the VP of Marketing, and Mr. Shepard, the VP of Sales, compete with each other for ratings; they need to change so they can cooperate for the optimization of the system. The System of Profound Knowledge will help them understand the issues involved and define the behavioral changes that are necessary to proceed with the transformation.

Prong Two: Daily Management

Prong two symbolizes the development, standardization, control, improvement, and innovation of methods (processes) used by employees in their daily routine. The development, standardization, and control of methods is called housekeeping. Housekeeping is accomplished through the Standardize-Do-Study-Act (SDSA) cycle. The SDSA cycle is a tool that helps employees document a process by creating an identity for the process.

It includes the following steps:

1. Standardize—Employees study a process and develop a "best practice" method, using tools such as flowcharts

2. Do—Employees conduct planned experiments on the "best practice" method on a trial basis

3. Study—Employees examine the results of the planned experiments

4. Act—Managers establish the standardized "best practice" method and formalize it through training.

The improvement and innovation of "best practice" methods is called daily management. The reader is cautioned that daily management is used in two different contexts in this book. First, it describes developing, standardizing, deploying, maintaining, improving, and innovating the methods required for daily work. Second, it describes only the maintenance, improvement, and innovation of methods for daily work. Daily management is accomplished through the Plan-

A Model for Quality Management

Do-Study-Act (PDSA) cycle. The PDSA cycle is a method that can aid management in improving and innovating processes. It guides management in reducing the difference between customers' needs and process performance.

The PDSA cycle consists of four basic stages:

1. Plan—Employees develop a plan to improve or innovate a "best practice" method, using tools such as a revised flow chart

2. Do—Employees test the plan, using planned experiments on a small scale or trial basis

3. Study—Employees study the effects of the experiment

4. Act—Employees take corrective actions. These corrective actions can lead to a new or modified plan or a revised "best practice" method, and are formalized through training. The PDSA cycle continues forever in an uphill progression of never-ending improvement

An example of housekeeping is developing a "best practice" route (method) for driving to work. The day before you drive to a new job, you plan your initial route (Standardize). The next morning you actually drive the route in rush hour and experience the traffic patterns (Do). You consider your route based on the traffic patterns and information from people at work who drive the route (Study). The next morning, you alter your route (Act).

You will continue daily management, using the PDSA cycle until you come to an optimal "best practice" route. The "best practice" route will include contingencies depending on weather, road improvement work, and special events.

Prong Three: Cross-Functional Management

The purpose of cross-functional management is to develop, standardize, control, improve, and innovate organizational methods across divisions and departments. This is carried out to optimize quality, cost, delivery, quantity, and safety. Management also considers the effects of the optimization on sales and profits.

Cross-functional management includes the following activities:

1. Developing, standardizing, controlling, improving, and innovating cross-functional methods.

2. Developing measurements for cross-functional methods.

3. Coordinating and optimizing cross-functional methods with department methods.

4. Allocating resources for cross-functional and department methods by establishing targets.

5. Ensuring that each department performs its deployed methods in daily management.

6. Monitoring cross-functional methods in respect to targets[5] from a corporate level.

---

5. Targets are used to allocate resources between methods.

7. Utilizing the PDSA cycle to decrease the difference between process performance and customer requirements.

Finally, as expertise is developed with cross-functional methods, they are moved into daily management methods.

The EC manages and coordinates all cross-functional project teams. All cross-functional teams serve two functions. First, they serve as an opportunity for team members to acquire macro-level process knowledge and to study and learn Dr. Deming's theory of management. Second, they provide an opportunity for team members to identify and resolve problems that cross department and division boundaries.

Blended families use cross-functional management to develop a viable family culture. When two people who have children from prior marriages form a family, it is difficult to coordinate and standardize the treatment of the children. The parents may have different goals, values, and methods in dealing with their own youngsters. When the family is blended, it has to look for ways to define cross-familial issues and resolve them successfully.

For example, the Doles, a blended family, have an issue to deal with. Mrs. Dole has an eight-year-old daughter, Janis, who goes to bed at 9:00 p.m. Mr. Dole's ten-year-old son, Larry, has the same bedtime. Larry questions his having the same bedtime as his eight-year-old stepsister. To resolve this issue, Mr. and Mrs. Dole have to discuss bedtimes and coordinate and improve their methods, taking into account the interaction between the former family units (departments).

Prong Four: Policy Management

Prong four represents policy management. Policy management is performed by using the PDSA cycle to improve and innovate the methods responsible for the difference between corporate performance and customer needs and wants, or to change the direction of an organization. Policy management assumes that housekeeping, daily management, and cross-functional management are functioning in the organization.

Policy management is accomplished through an interlocking system of committees. The Executive Committee (EC) is responsible for setting the strategic plan for the entire organization. It establishes values and beliefs, develops statements of vision and mission, and prepares a draft set of strategic objectives.

The Policy Deployment Committee (PDC) is responsible for deploying the strategic objectives throughout the entire organization. It develops an improvement plan (set of short-term tactics) for each department.

A Local Steering Team (LST) is responsible for implementing policy (short-term tactics) within a department, by coordinating and managing project teams. Project teams implement policy through improvement and innovation of the processes highlighted for attention. The management system is improved with each successive policy management cycle.

Policy management is used in family systems. Mr. and Mrs. Harris, EC of the Harris family, have a discussion. They would like to improve their family life with their children (mission). They decide that they should spend more time with the children (strategic objective).

They talk to their children about their objective to spend more time together (deploying the strategic objective). They propose eating dinner together on weekdays (short-term tactic). Each member of the family looks at his or her schedule, and they agree on the days that they are all free (implementing short-term tactics). They agree to try this system out for a week. Then they will meet and discuss how it might be improved in subsequent weeks.

Detailed View of the Model

The Detailed Fork Model is a detailed view of the Quality Management model presented in Figure 1.1. The detailed model includes 34 steps and is discussed in the remaining chapters of this book.

Summary

Chapter 1 presents an overview of the "Model for Total Quality Management" that is the focus of this book. The model integrates Dr. W. Edwards Deming's theoretical "System of Profound Knowledge" and the empirical "Total Quality Control" of the Japanese.

25

Understanding the System of Profound Knowledge encourages leaders of organizations to give up existing ideas of management and adopt a perspective that embraces the new paradigms: manage to create a win-win environment, manage to create intrinsic motivation, manage with a long-term process and results orientation, and manage to promote cooperation.

Understanding Japanese TQC allows leaders to use highly developed administrative systems, based on the experiences of what works in Japanese companies. Administrative systems include education, training and self-improvement; daily management; cross-functional management; and policy management.

The model presented in this book is one possible model of total quality management. Its purpose is to stimulate leaders to develop their own models, based on the "personality" of their particular organization and the needs of their shareholders.

The model is shaped like a fork with a handle and four prongs. The handle is "management's commitment to transformation." The first prong is "management's intellectual and emotional education." The second prong is "daily management." The third prong is "cross-functional management," and the fourth prong is "policy management." A short description of these areas was included in this chapter. Subsequent chapters will provide an in-depth discussion of each of the parts of the model.

Appendix 1

A Brief Discussion of the System of Profound Knowledge

In 1993, Dr. Deming published the System of Profound Knowledge in *The New Economics: For Industry, Government, Education,* MIT Center for Advanced Engineering Studies (Cambridge, MA) 1993, pp. 94-118. It comprises four components: appreciation of a system, theory of variation, theory of knowledge, and psychology. All four components are interdependent and will not stand alone. Fortunately, it is not necessary to be expert in any of the components to understand and apply the System of Profound Knowledge. This discussion is not meant to be complete; its purpose is to present some of the highlights of Dr. Deming's theory.

Appreciation of a System

A system is a collection of components that interact and have a common purpose (aim). It is the job of top management to optimize the entire system toward its aim. It is the responsibility of the management of the components of the system to promote the aim of the entire system; this may require that they suboptimize their component.

Theory of Variation

Variation is inherent in all processes. There are two types of causes of variation, special causes and system causes. Special causes of variation are external to the system. It is the responsibility of local people and engineers to determine and resolve special causes of variation. System causes of variation are due to the inherent design and structure of the system; they define the system. It is the responsibility of management to isolate and reduce system causes of variation.

27

A system which does not exhibit special causes of variation is stable; that is, it is a predictable system of variation. Its output is predictable in the near future.

There are two types of mistakes that can be made in the management of a system. First, treating a system cause of variation as a special cause of variation; this is by far the more common of the two mistakes—it is called tampering and will invariably increase the variability of the output of a system. The second type is treating a special cause of variation as a system cause of variation. Dr. Walter Shewhart developed the control chart to provide an economic rule for minimizing the loss from both types of mistakes.

Management requires knowledge about the interactions between the components of a system and its environment. Interactions can be positive or negative; they must be managed.

Theory of Knowledge

Information, no matter how speedy or complete, is not knowledge. Knowledge is indicated by the ability to predict future events with the risk of being wrong and the ability to explain past events without fail. Knowledge is developed by stating a theory, using the theory to predict a future outcome, comparing the observed outcome with the predicted outcome, and supporting, revising, or even abandoning the theory.

There is no true value of anything. Communication is possible when people share operational definitions.

Experience is of no value without the aid of theory. Theory allows people to understand and in-

28

terpret experience. It allows people to ask questions and to learn.

Psychology

Psychology helps us understand people, the interactions between people, and the interactions between people and the system of which they are part. Management must understand the difference between intrinsic motivation, extrinsic motivation, and over-justification. All people require different amounts of intrinsic and extrinsic motivation. It is the job of a manager to learn the proper mix of the two types of motivation for each of his people.

Management's Commitment to Transformation 2

Starting Quality Management

Total Quality Management is a never-end-ing journey. However, all journeys begin with one step. The moment the leadership of an organization takes that first step, the organization has started total quality man-agement. The time required to complete the process described in this model de-pends on the resources allocated to the process.

The best time to begin quality manage-ment is now. Like a person who wants to lose weight and finds reasons not to start a diet, organizations manufacture excuses

Purpose of this Chapter

Before any total quality management efforts can be undertaken, the top management of an organization has to make a commitment to transformation. The purpose of this chapter is to explain what is required to stimulate, sustain, coordinate, and promote that commitment.

A Model for the Transformation of an Organization

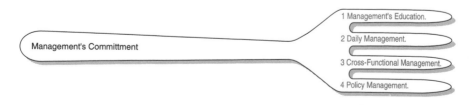

Figure 2.1

to put off the transformation. There is no specific time that is better than another to begin total quality management.

Aids to Promoting Total Quality Management

Different needs and situations stimulate an organization to pursue quality. Some examples of aids that promote the transformation of an organization to quality management include the desire to:

1. Exceed customer requirements
2. Improve the organization's image
3. Increase market size
4. Improve employee morale
5. Create a common mission
6. Improve communication
7. Standardize processes
8. Create best processes
9. Improve the physical environment
10. Resolve problems before they become crises
11. Bridge responsibility gaps
12. Improve the documentation of processes, products, and services
13. Improve the design of processes, products, and services
14. Improve manufacturing and delivery of service
15. Produce uniform products, at low cost and suited to the market

Barriers to Total Quality Management

What stops an organization from pursuing quality? Examples of barriers that hinder the transformation of management of an organization include:

1. Inability to change the mind set (paradigms) of top management

2. Inability to maintain momentum for the transformation
3. Lack of uniform management style
4. Lack of long-term corporate direction
5. Inability to change the culture of the organization
6. Lack of effective communication
7. Lack of discipline required to transform
8. Fear of scrutiny by supervisor
9. Fear of process standardization
10. Fear of loss of individualism
11. Fear of rigidity
12. Lack of financial and human resources
13. Lack of training and education
14. Lack of management commitment

Top Management's Reluctance to Commit

Lack of management commitment will stop a quality management effort before it begins. If transformation promises improvement in all areas of the organization, why isn't it embraced by all top managers? One reason may be that many managers in the United States are unfamiliar with company-wide success stories based on quality management theory. Leaders may be uncomfortable with this and show disdain for an unproven theory. They are unwilling to take the leap of faith toward what is perceived as a passing fad.

Top managers may not be pro-quality management because it is not their own creation. On the other hand, they may fear failure to meet short-term goals or to manage effectively. Leaders are reluctant to change because they have been personally successful. The organization under them may be falling apart, but as long as they continue to get raises and positive performance appraisals, they can deny the rampant problems.

Leaders who verbally promote quality management but impede quality management by their actions create a situation called "the slow death." The slow death is similar to a plant whose leaves (workers), branches (supervisors), and trunk (middle management) have a natural inclination to grow, but the gardener (top management) does not provide water. Over time, the plant will die, as will quality management, without the necessary nourishment of top management.

Responding to a Crisis

Top management creates and directs the energy necessary to transform an organization. There are only two known sources for this energy, a crisis or a vision[1] (see steps 1 and 2 of the Detailed Fork Model).

Many companies begin a program of quality management as a reaction to crises discovered by top management. This section describes the crises in three companies, two Japanese and one American, which led to their embarking on quality management. They all successfully resolved their crises using quality management.

---

1.   Kano, Noriaki, "A Perspective on Quality Activities in American Firms," *California Management Review*, Spring 1993, pp. 14-15.

JUKI Corporation

JUKI Corporation is a Japanese manufacturer of products ranging from sewing machines to industrial robots. In 1973, JUKI management uncovered external and internal crises, which led them to exert the energy necessary to make quality happen. The external crises included:

1. An inability to be competitive due to low quality and productivity

2. Union problems

The internal crises included:

1. Using the genius approach to R and D. JUKI management relied on the creative abilities of employees to generate new products. This process did not allow management to predict, with any degree of accuracy and dependability, new improvements and innovations in products and services.

2. Behaving with a market-out point of view. JUKI management created an organization in which products were produced and sold without determining the needs of customers.

3. Depending on the skill of individual workers to get the job done. JUKI management relied on the non-replenishable uniqueness of each individual to get jobs done, as opposed to standardizing work methods through training so that all relevant employees could do a particular job.

4. Acting as fire fighters. JUKI employees reacted to crises; they did not proactively improve processes to prevent crises from occurring in the future.

JUKI Corporation challenged for, and won, the Deming Prize in 1976.

CHAPTER *2*   Management's Commitment to Transformation

Kansai Electric Power Company

Kansai Electric Power Company is the power and electric utility for Kansai, Japan. In 1981, KEPCO management discovered several crises, which made them exert the energy necessary to make quality happen. These crises included:

1. An unacceptably high level of accidents in nuclear plants
2. A weak yen in respect to the dollar
3. An oil price that was high due to the OPEC pricing mechanism.

KEPCO challenged for, and won, the Deming Prize in 1984.

Florida Power & Light Company

Florida Power & Light Company (FP&L) is the largest utility furnishing the generation, transmission, distribution, and sale of electricity in the state of Florida. It experienced steady growth throughout its history. However, the pace of this growth increased dramatically between 1946 and 1974, making it difficult for FP&L's leaders to plan, finance, construct, and operate the utility. As FP&L grew, so did its managerial processes, becoming ever more cumbersome and unresponsive to customer needs. Nevertheless, because FP&L had been able to maintain stable prices for its customers it had avoided any potential crises.

In 1974, FP&L's ability to control costs was severely curtailed. In that year, OPEC's oil embargo and the subsequent increase in oil prices sent shock waves through the economy. Higher fuel prices quickly resulted in high inflation and declining sales growth. These external factors caused FP&L's stock price to fall as bond rates increased. Furthermore, in reaction to the oil crisis, the Federal government passed the National Energy Act, which resulted in competition for utilities and promotion of conservation.

"By the early 1980s, FP&L was facing a hostile environment created largely by high inflation, decreasing customer sales, rising electric rates, and increasing fuel oil prices. The price of electricity was increasing faster than the Consumer Price Index (CPI)."[2] At the same time, competitive pressures were beginning to affect FP&L's long-term prospects. Customer dissatisfaction grew along with increasing expectations for reliability, safety, and customer service. In the meantime, FP&L's inability to react quickly to new environmental demands worsened its situation.

Florida Power & Light Company challenged for, and won, the Deming Prize in November 1989.

In all of the above cases, top management uncovered crises that caused them to make a strong commitment to quality management and provide the leadership necessary to create quality.

Creating a Crisis

Top management can uncover and bring to the forefront the real or potential crises that face an organization. One method top management can use to create a crisis is asking a probing question, such as, "What are the quality requirements of our major product/service demanded by our major users/customers?" Frequently, top management is unable to answer this question. This may

---

2. From FPL Corporate document, "Description of Quality Improvement Program QIP—Corporate," Dec. 1988, p. 8.

create a crisis for top managers, if they realize that they are out of touch with their customers' needs.

Another method by which top management can create a crisis is by performing a SWOT (organizational **S**trengths and **W**eaknesses, and environmental **O**pportunities and **T**hreats) analysis. SWOT analyses can be helpful in determining the internal and external conditions and situations that face an organization.

A SWOT analysis is conducted through the following actions. First, understand the history, development, and growth of the organization over time. This requires analyzing the events that were most essential for the development and growth of the organization. Events could include selection of new products or services, selection of market segmentation strategies, and/or development of values and beliefs.

Next, identify the organization's internal strengths and weaknesses. This involves taking all the events in the organization's history and analyzing them to develop a list of the strengths and weaknesses of the organization. Areas of possible strengths or weaknesses are the values and beliefs of employees, philosophy and skills of management, knowledge and training of employees, hiring, training, and supervisory processes, methods for improvement and innovation of processes, and methods for exceeding customer requirements.

Third, identify the organization's external opportunities and threats. This involves studying the barriers to new entry in the industry, the degree of cooperation between members of the industry, the degree of trust and loyalty between customers and the members of the industry, the degree of trust and loyalty with suppliers and the members of the industry, the closeness of substitute products and/or services for the industry today and tomorrow, and the state of quality management technology in the industry. Examples of possible opportunities are improving and innovating products and services for existing and future market segments, decreasing costs and increasing productivity through the technology of quality management, and reducing rivalry and increasing cooperation between the members of an industry. Examples of possible threats are members of the industry developing improved technology that is proprietary and the enhanced attractiveness of substitute products and/or services to the customers in an industry.

Then, having studied the history of the organization, its internal strengths and weaknesses, and its external opportunities and threats, top management performs the SWOT analysis. This involves analyzing all the data collected and using it to understand the crises that face the organization.

All of the information about crises facing the organization is synthesized by top management. Top management then communicates this information about the real or potential crises throughout their interdependent system of stakeholders, to encourage the members to commit to the transformation.

Creating a Vision

Top management initiates action for the transformation via a crisis or a vision (see step 3 of the Detailed Fork Model). A vision can stimulate top management to expend the energy needed to transform an organization. This idea is critical for organizations not faced by an impending crisis. A vision can replace a crisis as a rallying point for the creation of quality. An important job of top management is to create a vision for the organization.

An example of a vision that drove top management to transform an organization is a situation that occurred in a social service agency. The agency, a group home program for troubled teenagers, was achieving its mission, adequately providing temporary shelter and basic care for adolescents separated from their families. However, the top management of the agency knew, through surveys of clients and referral agents, that the program needed to change to provide other services. These services included individual, group and family therapy, academic counseling, and an overall plan coordinated by the clients, along with social workers, psychologists, houseparents, teachers, and other involved staff members.

Top management had a vision of transforming the agency to one in which the needs of the clients were met in a more professional manner, utilizing a team to carry out an integrated plan. There was no crisis that stimulated this transformation. Top management saw a need to change

40

the organization to exceed the clients' needs, which were not being addressed by the program in its current state.

Once top management has established a vision for an organization and its interdependent system of stakeholders, it can utilize the methods discussed earlier to determine the issues that will prohibit realization of the vision.

Taking Action to Begin Total Quality Management

Retaining
Outside Counsel

After management has made the commitment to transformation, the first action is retaining outside counsel (see step 4 of the Detailed Fork Model). Outside counsel is necessary for two reasons. First, expertise in the System of Profound Knowledge is not likely to be found within an organization. Second, organizations frequently cannot recognize their own deficiencies; that is, they don't know what they don't know.

Once outside counsel has been retained, a window of opportunity for the transformation opens (see step 5 of the Detailed Fork Model). The window of opportunity has an unspecified time limit which varies from organization to organization. If signs of transformation do not become obvious to the stakeholders of an organization, they will not believe that top management is serious about transformation, and the window of opportunity for transformation will begin to close. This is a common reason for the failure of quality management efforts in organizations.

An important role of outside counsel is to help top management assess the current status, and predict the future condition, of relevant stakeholders in respect to the transformation. They determine the "barriers against" and the "aids for" a fruitful transformation, at all levels within an organization and throughout the organization's interdependent system of stakeholders (see step 6 of the Detailed Fork Model).

Barriers and aids data may be collected using brainstorming and force field analysis techniques. Brainstorming is a technique used by a team to gather large amounts of creative input (including facts, opinions, guesses, and data) about the "forces for" and "forces against" transformation. Force field analysis is a technique related to brainstorming that collects and organizes the "forces for" (driving forces) and the "forces against" (restraining forces) transformation. "Forces for" move an organization toward transformation. "Forces against" block movement toward transformation. The "forces for" and "forces against" data are organized in separate lists. The lists encourage people to think about the different aspects of transformation and to develop action plans to promote a desired transformation. If the forces against transformation are stronger than the forces for transformation, change will not occur. Depending on how much stronger the forces for transformation are than the forces against transformation, some change will occur.

Taking Action to Begin Total Quality Management

Consider the practical example of "Losing Weight":[3].

Losing Weight		
Driving Forces		**Restraining Forces**
Health threat	←→	Lack of time
Cultural obsession with being thin	←→	Genetic traits
Plenty of thin role models	←→	Unsympathetic family and friends
Embarrassment	←→	Lack of money for exercise, etc.
Negative Self-Image	←→	Lack of interest
Positive attitude toward exercise	←→	Bad advice
Lack of temptation	←→	Years of bad eating habits
Clothes don't fit	←→	Amount of sugar in prepared foods

---

3. GOAL/QPC, *The Memory Jogger: A Pocket Guide of Tools for Continuous Improvement*, 2nd Ed. (Methuen, MA), 1988, pp. 72-73.

The above force field analysis is useful to its author by helping him delineate the "forces for" and the "forces against" losing weight. As stated earlier, if the forces against losing weight are stronger than the forces for losing weight, no weight loss will occur. However, if the converse is true, some weight loss will occur. How much is a function of how much stronger the forces for weight loss are in respect to the forces against weight loss.

The outside expert, in conjunction with top management, utilizes the prior analyses to develop a plan for the transformation of the organization (see step 7 of the Detailed Fork Model).

Forming the Executive Committee

The top management forms an Executive Committee (EC), which consists of all policy makers in the organization. The chairman of the EC is the President or Chief Executive Officer of the organization (see step 8 of the Detailed Fork Model). The objective of the EC is to carry out the plan for transformation. This is accomplished by educating all members of the EC, as well as the members of the Board of Directors and stockholders (to the extent possible). Education and training includes Introduction to Dr. Deming's theory of management (the System of Profound Knowledge, the 14 points, and the deadly diseases), Psychology of the Individual and Team, Basic Quality Control Tools, and Administrative Systems for Quality (see step 9 of the Detailed Fork Model). Training in the administrative systems for quality management includes developing competence in daily management, cross-functional management, and policy management. These last three forms of management will be discussed in Chapters 4, 5, and 6, respectively.

The EC develops a plan to communicate transformation activities to all relevant stakeholders. Methods of communication can include preparing a newsletter highlighting transformation efforts, holding weekly briefing sessions on quality-related issues, and/or conducting yearly state of the organization addresses that discuss quality topics. Communications about transformation activities continue indefinitely into the future.

Once stakeholders receive appropriate communications concerning transformation activities, the members of the EC develop a plan to educate relevant stakeholders, including the Board of Directors, in respect to the transformation. This may require some degree of ingenuity. Furthermore, the members of the EC develop a plan to introduce and train all employees, subcontractors, and suppliers in the model for transformation.

Window of Opportunity

Once the above phase of education and training is complete, the window of opportunity for the transformation begins to close unless the members of the EC exhibit concrete signs of transformation to relevant stakeholders (see step 10 of the Detailed Fork Model). These signs include:

1. Entering a period of study (see step 11 of the Detailed Fork Model)

2. Selecting initial process improvement leaders in the departments (see step 14 of the Detailed Fork Model)

3. Selecting initial cross-functional process improvement projects to address issues

concerning transformation that span departments within the organization (see step 21 of the Detailed Fork Model)

4.   Conducting an initial presidential review of the policy of the organization (see step 28 of the Detailed Fork Model)

Questions for Self-Examination

The following questions can be helpful in stimulating discussion in an organization that is considering a transformation to total quality management.

1.   Can total quality management succeed without the commitment of your top management?

2.   Is it necessary to accept all of the paradigms of total quality management to start quality management? What are they?

3.   Can your organization ease into total quality management?

4.   What are some barriers that hinder the transformation of your organization to total quality management?

5.   What are some aids that promote the transformation of your organization to total quality management?

6.   Are there different approaches to total quality management? What are they? How do they differ?

7.   Is total quality management a fad?

8.   Does total quality management apply to the service aspects of your organization?

9.   Will our workers buy into total quality management?

10.   Will our unions buy into total quality management?

11.   How much training is needed for total quality management, by level?

12.   How much education is needed for total quality management, by level?

13.   How much will total quality management cost? Is it possible to compute this figure?

14.   How long will it take to have total quality management in our organization?

15.   When is the best time to begin total quality management?

16.   Can another organization's total quality management process become the blueprint for our organization's total quality management process?

17.   Is it helpful to visit organizations with successful total quality management processes?

Summary

Chapter 2 presents a discussion of "The Handle" of the fork model for total quality management that is presented in this book. "The Handle" is management's commitment to transformation, without which there can be no transformation. Aids to promoting total quality management and barriers to it are presented. Lack of management commitment is a barrier that is addressed in this chapter.

Top management's reluctance to commit to total quality management is discussed, and the authors postulate several reasons for it, including: U.S. managers who are unaware of success stories of total quality management, discomfort with what is viewed as an unproven theory, unwillingness to take a leap of faith toward what is perceived as a passing fad, and fear of failure.

There are only two known sources for the energy needed by top management to transform an organization: a crisis or a vision. Three cases are presented that demonstrate how companies responding to crises were stimulated to begin a process of quality management. These companies are JUKI (a Japanese manufacturer), Kansai Electric Power Company of Japan, and Florida Power & Light Company.

If a company is not currently faced with a crisis, top management can uncover and bring to the forefront the real or potential crises that exist. This can be done by asking the question presented in Chapter 2, or by using a SWOT (organizational **S**trengths and **W**eaknesses, and environmental **O**pportunities and **T**hreats) analysis, also discussed in the chapter.

Another way in which top management can begin the transformation is by creating its own vision as a rallying point for the introduction of quality. This is critical for organizations that are not facing a crisis.

After top management makes the commitment to transformation, the first action is retaining outside counsel, because an expert in the System of Profound Knowledge will not likely be "in-house," and the organization frequently can't recognize its own deficiencies. Outside counsel helps top management determine the "barriers against" and "aids for" transformation, and works with top management to develop a plan for the transformation.

Next, top management forms an Executive Committee (EC), which consists of all policy makers in the organization. The EC carries out the plan for transformation. Unless the members of the EC exhibit signs of transformation to relevant stakeholders, the window of opportunity for the transformation begins to close.

Questions for self-examination are presented at the end of Chapter 2, to stimulate thought and discussion in an organization that is contemplating transformation to quality management.

Prong One

M anagement's Fears About Education and Self-improvement

Education and self-improvement are both exciting and frightening processes. Top managers who have decided to become involved in these processes look forward to and fear them. They are anxious to learn about themselves and the improvement process, but they also have several concerns. Some questions they may be pondering are:

Purpose of this Chapter

After the top management of an organization commits to transformation, its members enter a period of education and self-improvement. The purpose of Prong One is to explain what top management needs to do to promote and coordinate its intellectual and emotional development in respect to transformation.

A Model for the Transformation of an Organization

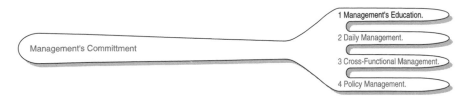

Management's Committment

1 Management's Education.

2 Daily Management.

3 Cross-Functional Management.

4 Policy Management.

Figure 3.1

1. What actually happens in these meetings?
2. Will I lose power?
3. Will I be embarrassed?
4. Will I look stupid?
5. Will I "get it"?
6. Will I be able to do it?
7. Will I have to change my personality?
8. Will I be exposed as incompetent?
9. Will I have to justify myself to the others?

These fears and questions are a natural reaction to the task that lies ahead of top management. Education and self-improvement are difficult, soul-searching activities that have a profound effect on the individual and the organization. It takes courage and strength of character to involve oneself in these processes. The guidance of an outside expert and the support of colleagues who share the same concerns will be very valuable during this arduous process.

Education and Self-Improvement Groups

One of the first tasks of the EC is forming one or more "education, training, and self-improvement" groups (see step 11 in the Detailed Fork Model). The aim of each group is to expand and deepen its understanding of the System of Profound Knowledge, the 14 points, the deadly diseases, and the practice of quality management as they relate to business and life.

A group contains between three and six members, and meets frequently (e.g., weekly). The areas of concentration are studying the System of Profound Knowledge, answering prescribed questions on total quality management using group consensus, designating study teams for each of the 14 points, and identifying and resolving personal barriers to transformation.

Studying the System of Profound Knowledge

The System of Profound Knowledge is discussed by the group, under the tutelage of an expert. The expert creates an environment in which group members deepen their understanding of how the System of Profound Knowledge might affect organizational and personal decision-making.

The expert may use role-playing, case studies, or workshops to generate the individualized feedback necessary for each top manager so that he or she can transform personally and consequently promote the transformation of the organization.

The purpose of this type of session is not to "mess with" anybody's personal beliefs and values, but rather to make them aware of an alternative system of beliefs (the System of Profound Knowledge) and its potential impact on them and their decision-making processes.

An example of a group meeting in which the concepts of the System of Profound Knowledge are being discussed is presented below. The group consists of the QM EXPERT, the CEO of the company, BOB, the VP of Sales, CAROL, the VP of Production, TED, and the VP of Quality, ALICE.

Discussion

QM EXPERT: Last time we were in the middle of a heated debate about intrinsic versus extrinsic motivation. I'd like to continue that discussion. Carol, you were having a hard time figuring out how you were going to motivate your people without sales incentives.

CAROL: I still am. I've been thinking about it a lot. Some of my people will do a good job, even without the awards, but there are others who need that carrot to get them going.

TED: I know what you mean. I feel the same way, except it's worse in Production. If I don't reward them for output, they'll just slack off.

QM EXPERT: Alice, what are your feelings?

ALICE: I agree with Dr. Deming's theory, but I'm at a loss as to what can replace our incentives. I understand Carol and Ted's concerns.

QM EXPERT: Bob, what do you think about what you're hearing?

BOB: I feel pretty much the same way, but I guess we have to try and look at it differently. We need to address everyone's concerns, and at the same time, we have to be looking for ways to change our system to be more in line with the direction we're going in.

Discussion *(Continued)*

QM EXPERT: I feel that we're making some progress. Everyone seems open to some more information about alternative action. Last time you weren't as receptive. Let's get into how we can create joy in work at your company, without relying on extrinsic rewards. We'll start with each of you telling us what motivates you to do your job. Bob, let's hear from you first.

BOB: Well, I have to tell you that I enjoy getting my pay check. (Everyone laughs.) But that's an extrinsic motivator.

QM EXPERT: I appreciate your honesty, Bob. Nobody expects you to work for no pay. But I'm sure there are other things that make you get up and come to work.

BOB: Sure, I love what I do. It's a challenge running this company. I have to be on my toes, always thinking, planning, and learning. It's exciting watching my ideas get played out, especially when they work. I like mentoring people, watching them grow and develop. Do you want me to keep going?

Discussion *(Continued)*

QM EXPERT: Actually, that's enough for now. You've given us a lot to work with. All the motivators that Bob mentioned, aside from his pay check, of course, were intrinsic. Our task now is to transform the organization so that each and every employee in it can experience the same positive feelings about work that Bob has expressed. What I'd like to do now is some role playing. Ted, I want you to pretend that you're one of the line workers in your department, Sam, reporting for his shift. Alice, I want you to be Ted.

TED (as SAM): Good morning, Mr. Lawrence.

ALICE (as TED): Hi Sam. No time for chit-chat this morning. We've got to get to work to fill the Dynamic order that just came in.

TED (as SAM): That might be a problem. The sorter was giving us a problem yesterday. Unless the night shift took care of it, it's going to have to be down for awhile.

ALICE (as TED): Why didn't you tell Jim yesterday?

TED (as SAM): I tried to see Jim, but he was in a meeting with you the whole afternoon.

QM EXPERT: Let's stop right there. Ted, what were you experiencing?

	Discussion (Continued)
TED:	I was feeling bad and getting angry. First, the guy barely says good morning to me. Then he starts blaming me for something that's not my fault.
CAROL:	I think we all do that to the line workers. When we're under pressure, we take everything out on them.
BOB:	When you think about it, why would they want to come to work? No wonder we have such a high absentee rate.
QM EXPERT:	I think we're really onto something here. If we can make working at Universal a more positive experience for all employees, we can begin to create intrinsic motivation for everyone, not just Bob.

The above example demonstrates the role of the QM expert and the desired atmosphere of the group setting. The QM expert is supportive, and provides continuity from one meeting to the next. He or she creates a nonjudgmental atmosphere in which group members are comfortable to express themselves. The QM expert includes everyone in the group in discussions and uses the leader as a role model for the others. The expert praises the group for growth and gently pushes the members when they are at an impasse. He or she summarizes where the group is going next and identifies the task in relation to the transformation.

Answering Prescribed Questions on Quality Management

The group prepares, in writing, answers to an appropriate subset of the 66 questions in Chapter 5 of Dr. Deming's book, *Out of the Crisis*.[1] It is important that group members reach consensus on the answers to each of the questions so they have a uniform understanding of what quality means within their organization and learn participatory management skills.

Group members follow the PDSA cycle in this endeavor, and they spend at least two hours per week discussing each question. One hour is devoted to developing a plan (PLAN) for collecting the data required to answer the question and establishing a team to collect said data. Next, the plan is carried out (DO) by group members. The results are studied (STUDY) by group members, who then spend at least one more hour discussing the answer to each question. The group facilitator writes up the consensual answer to each question (ACT).

The written answer is sent to an external expert in Dr. Deming's theory of management so that he or she may use it as a basis for guiding the group's education and self-improvement process. That is, the expert will use the written answer to help group members establish an improved PLAN for understanding the question

---

1. This method for educating top management was pointed out to the authors by William Latzko, Bergen County, New Jersey. The 66 questions for self-examination can be found in Deming, W.E., *Out of the Crisis*, MIT CAES (Cambridge, MA) 1986, pp. 156-166.

under study. The two hours of study per week per question mentioned earlier represents an arbitrary amount of study time and should be modified in accordance with the progress of the group. The period of education and self-improvement should be extended indefinitely into the future (see step 12 of the Detailed Fork Model).

The following section is an example of correspondence between a Quality Management expert and members of an organization working on transformation. First, the initial letter sent by the outside counsel to begin the process of answering the prescribed questions is presented.

Letter

To: Alice Walters

VP, Quality

Universal Company

From: Quality Expert

Dear Alice:

I am glad to hear that Universal is going to begin the never-ending journey toward quality. The journey is long and difficult. Education is your guide.

Your organization's education in the area of the improvement of quality should begin with top management, Bob and his immediate staff reports. The more top management studies the philosophy and techniques for the improvement of quality, the quicker Universal will progress on its journey toward quality.

Letter *(Continued)*

Initially, this education will require that top management meet weekly to discuss and prepare in writing answers to the 66 questions in Chapter 5 of Dr. Deming's book, *Out of the Crisis*. It is important that top management come to consensus in respect to the answers to each of the 66 questions so they have a uniform understanding of what quality means at Universal and improve their participatory management skills.

Top management should plan to spend at least two hours per week discussing each question, using the PDSA cycle in this endeavor. One hour is devoted to developing a plan (PLAN) for collecting the data required to answer the question and establishing a team to collect said data. Next, the plan is carried out (DO) by team members. The results are studied (STUDY) by top management. Management spends at least one more hour discussing the answer to each question. The Executive Committee facilitator writes up the consensus answer to each question (ACT).

The written answer is sent to me so that I may use it as a basis for guiding management's education at the monthly meeting of the Executive Committee. I will use the written answer to help management establish an improved PLAN for understanding the question under study.

The two hours of study per week per question mentioned earlier represents an arbitrary amount of study time and will be modified in accordance with the educational progress of EC members.

If you have any questions, give me a call.

The following is the expert's response to the company's answers to the first of Dr. Deming's 66 questions in *Out of the Crisis*. Question one appears below for your convenience.

1a. Has your company established constancy of purpose?

1b. If yes, what is the purpose? If no, what are the obstacles?

1c. Will this stated purpose stay fixed, or will it change as presidents come and go?

1d. Do all employees in your company know about this stated constancy of purpose (*raison d'etre*), if you have formulated one?

1e. How many believe it to the extent that it affects their work?

1f. Whom does your president answer to? Whom do your board of directors answer to?

Letter

To: Alice Waters

VP, Quality

Universal Company

From: Quality Expert

Dear Alice:

Congratulations on taking a significant step towards the pursuit of quality.

Please explain to the Executive Committee the importance of not becoming frustrated by my extensive critique. My critique is not a judgement of their work; rather, it is an attempt to improve their education. The answer-critique-answer cycle is the method by which they will learn how to pursue quality.

CHAPTER **3** Management's Education (Prong One)

Letter *(Continued)*

Please remind them that the point of answering the questions and the critiques is education, not to get through all 66 questions. To that end, please find my critique in the form of questions and comments for your Executive Committee's written consensus answer to question 1 in Chapter 5 of Dr. Deming's book, *Out of the Crisis*.

General Comments (Prelude To Question 1)

Did your committee follow the PDSA cycle when answering question 1? Or did they just have a discussion (PLAN) and answer writing session (ACT), with no DO and STUDY?

1.   Did they develop a plan (PLAN) for collecting the data required to answer question 1 and establish a team to collect said data?

   a. If yes, where is the data?

   b. If no, why not?

2.   Did the duly appointed team carry out (DO) the PLAN?

3.   Did the duly appointed team study the results (STUDY) and report back to the Executive Committee?

   a. If the study phase yielded negative information, did the Executive Committee punish the team for bringing back unfavorable results?

   b. If the study phase yielded positive information, did the Executive Committee modify the organization's mission (ACT)?

Letter (Continued)

Comments on Question 1a

Has your company established constancy of purpose?

Your answer: "No."

You must not be frustrated by not having constancy of purpose after all of your work in this regard to date. The critical point is to build a clear vision, mission, set of values and beliefs, and strategic plan with tactics out of your current vision and mission statements, quality policy, company values, and strategic plan. Your problem is that you have not integrated the information you have. This causes conflict and confusion. This conflict and confusion will grow greater as you move down in the organization due to interpretation and reinterpretation of the mission.

Universal's vision is an ideal state that employees can pursue, even though they may never get there. The mission is the vehicle by which employees will pursue their vision. The values set the boundaries on employees' behavior in their pursuit of the vision via the mission. Finally, the mission, in conjunction with your values and beliefs, sets the stage for management to establish strategies and tactics.

Comments on Question 1b

If yes, what is the purpose?

If no, what are the obstacles?

Your answer: The obstacles include:

Letter *(Continued)*

---

1. "We have communicated too many statements to employees.... Although these statements complement each other, there is no specific statement of constancy of purpose."

2. "...our actions do not support our words."

First, let me address the obstacle of communicating too many quality-related statements to employees, without a statement of constancy of purpose. The Executive Committee's resolve to this obstacle is that constancy of purpose will be achieved by communicating Universal's values and beliefs to all employees. In my opinion, a better approach would be to integrate your vision, mission, values and beliefs, strategies, and tactics so that they provide a clear road map to all employees when they are deployed throughout the organization.

To do this, the Executive Committee forms a cross-functional team. The basic question to be addressed by the team is: "What are the obstacles that prevent Universal from pursuing its vision and mission?" The team considers barriers to integrating the vision, mission, values and beliefs, strategies, and tactics when answering the above question.

Second, let me address the obstacle of management's actions not supporting management's words. Point one of Dr. Deming's 14 points addresses exactly this issue. Establishing constancy of purpose, through an integrated vision, mission, set of values, strategies, and tactics, is equivalent to establishing a desired nominal value for a process. Getting all employees to uniformly interpret and follow said purpose is a problem of the reduction of variation.

Letter *(Continued)*

One important job of the Executive Committee members is to manage, and get their people to manage, in respect to Universal's purpose. How you go about doing this is covered in Dr. Deming's points on training, supervision, and barriers to pride of workmanship. It is important that the quality expert keep working with the top management until they understand and exhibit the System of Profound Knowledge in the conduct of their daily work. When top management has made the transformation, the quality expert provides education and training throughout the organization.

Comments on Question 1c

Will this stated purpose stay fixed or will it change as presidents come and go?

Your answer: "By using Universal's values and beliefs, the purpose will not change."

The answer to question 1c is really unknown. Only a succession of presidents and time will tell the real story. However, the improvement process continues, assuming the answer to question 1c is "stay fixed."

Comments on Question 1d

Do all employees of your company know about this stated constancy of purpose, if you have formulated one?

Your answer: "All employees are familiar with Universal's values and beliefs. They probably do not recognize them as constancy of purpose."

Letter *(Continued)*

How do you know that the employees are familiar with the company's values? Where is the data? It is important that you manage by theory and facts, not by unsubstantiated opinion and guesswork.

Further, a newsletter, if you don't already have one, is extremely helpful in communicating your purpose and plans to employees. The newsletter is also an excellent vehicle for education and training.

Comments on Question 1e

How many believe it to the extent that it affects their work?

Your answer: "...a small number..."

How do you know that the company's values and beliefs affect only a small number of employees in the way they perform their jobs? Where is the data? In what ways do the company's values and beliefs affect the way employees do their jobs? Are these effects positive or negative? Do you have any data to explain these effects? What are the characteristics of employees who are affected? Not affected? What explains the difference? This data may help the Executive Committee develop a plan to spread Universal Company's values to all employees.

Comments on Question 1f

Whom does your president answer to?

Whom does your board of directors answer to?

Your answer: "Customers and employees."

Letter *(Continued)*

I agree. Ultimately, the president and the board of directors answer to customers and employees. If your customers do not experience joy with your products and services, which are the result of the decision-making process of the president and the board, they will not give Universal the gift of business. Also, if your employees do not take pride in their work and joy in the outcome, they will not give Universal the energy required for a successful business. Clearly, this affects profit, return on investment, and dividends. Stockholders experience joy from the same set of managerial decisions.

The following discussion may shed some new light on your answer to question 1f. The old way of thinking about an organization is to visualize it as a pyramid in which decisions move from top management, through middle management, to line workers, and eventually to customers. In this type of pyramid, everyone's effort is focused on making the person(s) higher up in the pyramid (their boss) happy. This is fueled by administrative systems like performance appraisal. Please note that making your boss happy is very different from making your customer happy.

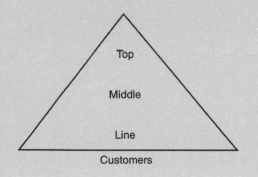

Letter *(Continued)*

A new way of thinking about an organization is to visualize it as an inverted pyramid in which decisions move from the base of customers, through line workers, through middle management, to top management, and then back up through the pyramid to customers. In this type of pyramid, everyone's effort is focused on making the person(s) higher up in the pyramid (their customer) happy. The president's job is to support top management, top management's job is to support middle management, and so on, throughout the organization. Please note that making customers and employees happy is what your president and board should be doing.

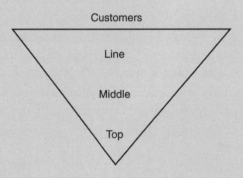

I hope my critique is helpful. If you have any questions, give me a call.

Designating Study Teams for Each of the Fourteen Points

The members of the EC create study teams for each of the 14 points. The job of each study team is to remove organizational barriers to the transformation in respect to its point, by studying and using the System of Profound Knowledge. The activities of each team may lead to the establishment of a cross-functional team (see step 21 of the Detailed Fork Model), an educational program for members of the EC (see step 12 of the Detailed Fork Model), or input into the policy management process (see step 29 of the Detailed Fork Model).

An example of a study team is one that is created to study point 12, "Remove barriers that rob employees of their pride of workmanship."[2] One of the barriers that is identified by the group is the company's performance appraisal system. The cross-functional team uses the System of Profound Knowledge as the basis for discussing, redesigning, and continuously improving the performance appraisal process. The case study of Field of Flowers, presented in Chapter 5, offers further information on study teams using the System of Profound Knowledge to redesign and improve systems that create barriers to transformation.

Identifying and Resolving Personal Barriers to Transformation

Each member of the EC identifies and resolves his or her issues that create barriers to the transformation (see step 13 of the Detailed Fork Model). Examples of individual barriers to the transformation are the following beliefs:

---

2. Deming, W. E., *Out of the Crisis*, MIT CAES (Cambridge, MA) 1986, p.77.

1. Extrinsic motivators bring out the best in people.

2. Focusing on results yields improvement of results.

3. Fire fighting will improve an organization in the long term.

4. Effective decisions can be made using guesswork and opinion.

5. Rational decision-making can be performed using only visible figures.

6. Quantity is inversely related to quality.

7. Your most important customer is your superior.

8. Management's function is to construct, execute, and control plans.

9. Competition is superior to cooperation, and winners and losers are necessary in any interaction.

Each member of the EC examines his or her own opinions to determine if he or she holds any of the above beliefs or others that would impede the transformation. The quality management expert can use the following questionnaire to pinpoint problem areas that individuals may be experiencing.[3]

Directions:

1. Below is a list of managerial traits which have been placed on a 0-10 scale.

---

3. McNary L., *The Deming Management Theory: A Managerial Leadership Profile for the New Economic Age*, Doctoral Dissertation (May 1993), The University of New Mexico (Albuquerque, NM). On microfilm with the University of Michigan (Ann Arbor, MI).

2. Place an "X" on each scale to indicate the degree to which *you exhibit* a particular trait in your daily management style.[4]

3. Remember, there are no right or wrong answers.

Managerial Traits	

A. With respect to employees, I believe in:

1	2	3	4	5	6	7	8	9	10

Fostering motivation through rewards and punishment	Neutral	Fostering motivation through pride and satisfaction in work

B. With respect to employees, I believe in:

1	2	3	4	5	6	7	8	9	10

Managing for the short term using daily production reports and/or quarterly measures of profit	Neutral	Managing for the long term by expanding the market for all

---

4. In Dr. McNary's dissertation this instruction reads as follows: "Place an 'X' on each scale to indicate the degree to which *you possess* a particular trait."

Managerial Traits *(Continued)*

C. In making any organizational decision, I believe in:

1	2	3	4	5	6	7	8	9	10

Focusing on the result of a process with an emphasis on numerical goals and quotas	Neutral	Focusing on the process to get results with an emphasis on improvement and innovation

D. I believe in:

1	2	3	4	5	6	7	8	9	10

Managing with a traditional hierarchical organizational chart	Neutral	Managing with an emphasis on customer-supplier relationships

E. For the success of my organization, I believe that:

1	2	3	4	5	6	7	8	9	10

Optimizing my own situation or competition is most important	Neutral	Optimizing the system of inter-dependent components or cooperation is most important

Managerial Traits *(Continued)*

F. With respect to employees, I believe in:

1	2	3	4	5	6	7	8	9	10

Managing by formal appraisal process	Neutral	Managing through informal feedback and coaching

G. I believe in:

1	2	3	4	5	6	7	8	9	10

Basing decisions on visible figures such as ROI calculations	Neutral	Basing decisions on operational definitions, visible figures, and considering the effect of invisible figures

H. I believe that:

1	2	3	4	5	6	7	8	9	10

Management cannot be responsible for all components of an organization	Neutral	Management is responsible for all components of an organization

Managerial Traits *(Continued)*

I. I believe that:

1	2	3	4	5	6	7	8	9	10

Management's job is planning, organizing, directing, and evaluating	Neutral	Management's job is prediction through understanding the capability of processes and people as well as the interaction between them

J. I believe that:

1	2	3	4	5	6	7	8	9	10

Managers should not necessarily be leaders	Neutral	Managers should be leaders

A leader who manages in accordance with Dr. Deming's theory of management will have a score of 10 on each of the above questions and a total score of 100 points. The closer a manager's score is to 0 for a given question, the less a manager exhibits an aptitude to lead in accordance with Dr. Deming's theory of management. A quality expert can use a manager's scores on the above questions to pinpoint the elements of the System of Profound Knowledge that a manager is having difficulty internalizing.

After identifying the specific areas in need of attention, the expert and individual manager meet to discuss why holding a particular belief is detrimental to transformation. In depth, private sessions may be necessary to understand the "whys" and "ramifications" of and "alternatives" to the above beliefs. The behaviors that these beliefs promote are also discussed, and ways of changing both attitudes and behaviors are suggested.

Identifying and resolving personal barriers is one of the most important areas in the transformation of an organization because it addresses the root cause of the most common reason for failure, lack of commitment on the part of top management. The following section presents an example of a private session between the quality management expert and Bob, the CEO of The Universal Company.

Discussion

QM EXPERT:	How do you think everyone is taking to the training?
BOB:	I think it's going very well.
QM EXPERT:	I agree. I wanted to meet with you individually because I thought I sensed an area that you're not entirely comfortable with.
BOB:	Let's get it out in the open. What is it?
QM EXPERT:	Promoting cooperation instead of competition.
BOB:	(thinks for a moment) You're pretty sharp.

Discussion *(Continued)*

QM EXPERT: That's what you pay me for. Anyway, it's an area that a lot of top guys have trouble with. After all, you got where you are by being the best you can and beating out other people. It follows that you want to keep competing, and encourage your people to do the same.

BOB: I guess.

QM EXPERT: When you were in high school did you play a sport?

BOB: Yeah, football.

QM EXPERT: Did you play varsity?

BOB: No, and I was miserable about it. I really wanted that letter, but the coach wouldn't put me on the team.

QM EXPERT: So you remember how it felt?

BOB: Like it was yesterday. I hated it.

QM EXPERT: What did you hate?

BOB: I was trying as hard as the guys who made the team. And, I'm not so sure the guys on the team were better than I was.

Discussion *(Continued)*	
QM EXPERT:	Exactly, that's Dr. Deming's point. Competition doesn't help anybody improve. It just creates winners and losers. Do you think you're creating this kind of situation anywhere for your people?
BOB:	I guess I am. We have an "Employee of the Month" contest. Only one person wins. I'm sure there are others who deserve to win, too. Their morale probably hits the floor when they don't win.
QM EXPERT:	I'm sure you're right. Now that you understand the downside of competition at a gut level, I know we'll be able to work on improvement in this area.
BOB:	Thanks for the feedback. I don't think I would have come to this by myself.
QM EXPERT:	That's what I'm here for. I'm glad I could help.

The Quality Management Leader

Top management's education and self-improvement includes group and individual study of the System of Profound Knowledge and the identification and resolution of personal barriers to transformation. Guided by an expert, the quality management leader will develop his or her management style to incorporate the attributes necessary to lead the organization.[5] The quality management leader should possess the following characteristics:

1.   A leader sees the organization as a system of interrelated components, each with an aim, but all focused collectively to support the aim of the system of interdependent stakeholders. This type of focus may require suboptimization of some components of the system.

2.   A leader tries to create for everybody interest and challenge, joy in work, and pride in the outcome. He or she tries to optimize the education, skills, and abilities of everyone, and helps everyone to improve. Improvement and innovation are his or her aim.[6]

3.   A leader coaches and trains, and does not judge and punish.[7] He or she creates security, trust, freedom, and innovation. A leader is aware that creation of trust requires that he or she take a risk.[8] A leader is an active listener and does not pass judgement on those to whom he or she listens.

4.   A leader has formal power, power from knowledge, and power from personality. A leader develops and utilizes the power from knowledge and personality when operating in an existing paradigm of manage-

5.   The attributes of a leader are taken from: Deming, W.E., *The New Economics* MIT CAES (Cambridge, MA), 1993, pp. 128-131.

6.   Deming, W.E., *The New Economics*, p. 128.

7.   Deming, W.E., *The New Economics*, p. 129.

8.   Carlisle and Parker, *Beyond Negotiation*, John Wiley and Sons, (1989).

ment. However, a leader may have to resort to the use of formal power when shifting from one paradigm of management to another.

5. A leader uses plots of points and statistical calculation with knowledge of variation, to try to understand both the leader's performance and that of his or her people. A leader is someone who knows when his or her people are experiencing problems that make their performance fall outside of the system and treats the problems as special causes of variation. These problems could be common-cause to the individual (long-term alcoholic) but special-cause to the system (alcoholic works differently from his peers).

6. A leader understands the benefits of cooperation and the losses from competition.[9]

7. He or she does not expect perfection.

8. A leader understands that experience without theory does not facilitate prediction of future events. For example, a leader cannot predict how a person will do in a new job based solely on experience in the old job. A leader has a theory to predict how an individual will perform in a new job.

9. A leader is able to predict the future to plan the actions necessary to pursue the organization's aim. Rational prediction of

9. Deming, W.E., *The New Economics*, p. 131 and Kohn, Alfie, *No Contest*, Houghton Mifflin (1986).

future events requires that the leader continuously work to create stable processes with low variation.

A manager who does not possess any or all of the above attributes will have problems with the transformation. Again, it may be necessary to arrange for private sessions between some members of the EC and an expert in Dr. Deming's theory of management to discuss in depth, and confidentially, the "whys" and "ramifications" of the above attributes. As with beliefs, this step may be critical to a successful transformation because it goes to the root cause of the most common reason for failing to transform an organization, lack of commitment on the part of top management.

Summary

Chapter 3 presents a discussion of Prong One of the fork model that is presented in this book. Prong One is management's intellectual and emotional education and self-improvement. After top management of an organization commits to transformation, its members enter a period of education and self-improvement. These are difficult, soul-searching activities that have a profound effect on the individual and the organization.

One of the first tasks of the EC is forming one or more education, training, and self-improvement groups which concentrate on the following areas:

1. Studying the System of Profound Knowledge

2.   Answering prescribed questions on quality management, using group consensus

3.   Designating study teams for each of the 14 points

4.   Identifying and resolving personal barriers to transformation

The System of Profound Knowledge is discussed by the group under the guidance of an expert. The expert creates an environment in which group members deepen their understanding of how the System of Profound Knowledge might affect organizational and personal decision-making. Chapter 3 provides an example of this type of group session, in dialogue form, to illustrate the role of the QM expert and the desired atmosphere of the group setting.

The second area in which a group can focus is answering, in writing, an appropriate selection of the 66 questions in Chapter 5 of Dr. Deming's book, *Out of the Crisis.* Group members reach consensus on their answers, and the answers are discussed with a QM expert. An example of this type of correspondence between a group and a QM expert is presented in Chapter 3.

Designating study teams for each of the 14 points is another task of the EC. The job of each study team is to remove organizational barriers to the transformation by studying and using the System of Profound Knowledge. An example is a study team that is working on point 12, "Remove barriers that rob employees of their pride of workmanship." The cross-functional team identifies the company's performance appraisal system as a barrier and uses the System of Profound Knowledge as the basis for discussing and redesigning the process.

The fourth area that is important in management's education and self-improvement is identifying and resolving personal barriers to transformation. Each member of the EC examines his or her opinions to determine if he or she holds any beliefs that would be detrimental to the transformation. The QM expert can use a questionnaire to help pinpoint problem areas that individuals may be experiencing.

Identifying and resolving personal barriers is one of the most important areas in the transformation because it addresses the root cause of the most common reason for failure, lack of commitment on the part of top management. In-depth, private sessions may be necessary between the QM expert and an individual manager. An example of such a session is provided in Chapter 3.

Characteristics of the quality management leader are discussed. Certain attributes are necessary if the leader hopes to transform an organization. Guided by an expert, the leader will develop these traits through the use of the methods presented in this chapter.

Prong Two

Selecting Initial Project Teams: Steps 14 Through 17

The members of the EC select initial Process Improvement Leaders (PILs) in the different departments of an organization (see step 14 of the Detailed Fork Model). PILs can be either full-time or part-time. The decision to have only full-time PILs, only part-time PILs, or both types of PILs depends on the needs of project teams.

Early in a transformation, an organization may need a greater proportion of full-time PILs. However, as the transformation proceeds, an organization may need a smaller

Purpose of this Chapter

The purpose of this chapter is to explain what is required to develop, standardize, deploy, maintain, improve, and innovate the methods required for daily work in all areas of an organization. Daily work is managed through "daily manage–ment," Prong Two of the model presented in this book (see Figure 4.1).

When top management is ready to begin transforming the organization, it needs concrete ways of translating theory into practice. Daily management is one of the vehicles top management uses to accomplish this task.

A Model for the Transformation of an Organization

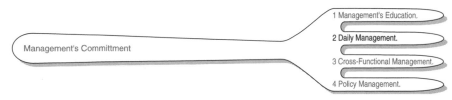

Management's Committment

1 Management's Education.

2 Daily Management.

3 Cross-Functional Management.

4 Policy Management.

Figure 4.1

proportion of full-time PILs. The change in the need for full-time PILs is due to an increase in the general level of "quality" knowledge in the organization and, consequently, a decrease in the need for the aid provided to project teams by full-time PILs.

PILs receive training in "Basic Quality Control Tools" and "Psychology of the Individual and Team" (see step 15 of the Detailed Fork Model). "Basic Quality Control Tools" explains how to:

1. Document and define a process

2. Draw samples from a process

3. Determine appropriate levels of measurement

4. Construct, use, and interpret Shewhart control charts

5. Detect and rectify out-of-control patterns

6. Diagnose a process using the basic quality control tools (flowcharts and training, brainstorming and cause and effect diagrams, check sheets, Pareto diagrams, histograms, run charts, scatter diagrams, and stratification)

7. Conduct process capability and process improvement studies[1]

"Psychology of the Individual and Team" explains how to:

---

1. One possible text for this course is Gitlow, H., Oppenheim, A., and Oppenheim, R., *Quality Management: Tools and Methods for Improvement*, 2nd ed., Richard D. Irwin, Inc. (Homewood, IL), 1995.

1. Apply individual psychology to manage the transformation

2. Learn techniques for improving employee satisfaction

3. Plan for total employee involvement

4. Promote empowerment of individuals and teams (more on this later)

5. Apply group psychology to establish and build teams[2]

Next, the members of the EC select the initial projects to be addressed by project teams (see step 16 of the Detailed Fork Model). Once the PILs and the projects have been determined, the members of the EC, in consultation with the PILs, select the members of each initial project team (see step 17 of the Detailed Fork Model). Project teams are formed with a specific purpose, consist of people from the same area (small unit), and exist in perpetuity. All project team members receive training in "Basic Quality Control Tools" and "Psychology of the Individual and Team" (see step 17 of the Detailed Fork Model).

Doing Daily Management: Step 18

Overview

After training, each initial project team works on one or more methods through daily management (see step 18 of the Detailed Fork Model). Daily management is develop-

2. One possible text for this course is Scholtes, P., *The Team Handbook*, Joiner Associates, 1991.

ing, standardizing, deploying, maintaining, improving, and innovating the methods required for daily work. The development, standardization, and deployment of methods for daily work is called housekeeping[3] because "it is a procedure which sets things in order."[4] The maintenance, improvement, and innovation of methods for daily work is simply called daily management. Once again, the reader is cautioned that daily management is used in two different contexts in this section. First, it describes developing, standardizing, deploying, maintaining, improving, and innovating the methods required for daily work. Second, it describes only the maintenance, improvement, and innovation of methods for daily work.

Housekeeping

The housekeeping functions of daily management are developed through a procedure called function deployment.[5] Function deployment requires that relevant employees determine what functions are required to perform each method needed in their daily work. Each function is subject to the scrutiny of the following questions:

---

3. The name "housekeeping" is taken from Total Productivity Maintenance (TPM). See Imai, Masaaki, *KAIZEN: The Key To Japan's Competitive Success*, (1986), Random House, New York, NY, pp. 158-159.

4. Quotation from Schultz, Louis, *Process Management International*, Minneapolis, MN, 1990.

5. Mizuno, Shigeru, *Company-Wide Quality Control*, Asian Productivity Organization, 4-14, Asasaka 8-chome, Minato-ku, Tokyo 107, Japan (1988), pp. 55-61.

1. *Why* is this function required?
2. *What* is this function intended to achieve? *What* is the aim of this function?
3. *What* resources are necessary for this function?
4. *What* target must be set to allocate appropriate resources to this function to optimize the aim of the organization?
5. *Where* in the process should this function take place?
6. *When* should this function be implemented? Carried out?
7. *Who* is responsible for this function?
8. *How* does this function contribute to the optimization of the system of interdependent stakeholders for the organization?
9. *What* measurements are used to monitor this function?
10. *How* will this function be carried out?
11. *Does* this function contain non-value-added steps?

Housekeeping is practiced through the SDSA cycle. The SDSA cycle has four stages: "STANDARDIZE," "DO," "STUDY," and "ACT." The Standardize stage involves teaching employees how to study and understand the causal factors that affect each critical method they work with (e.g., using flowcharts). The employees developing the best practice method use the flowchart to highlight non-value-added steps, and work toward eliminating them. Employees can also use other tools to understand the causal systems that affect their methods, such as cause and effect diagrams, interrelationship diagraphs, and simulations. All the employees who use a particular method compare notes on causal factors and develop one "best practice method," as seen through a "best practice" flowchart.

At this stage, question 11 can be addressed by using an integrated flowchart. This type of flowchart adds at least one dimension to a typical flowchart. An example of an integrated flowchart with one extra dimension is shown in Figure 4.2. The non-value-added steps are shaded in grey.

An integral part of preparing a "best practice" method is developing measurements to monitor the "best practice" method. Measurements can yield data that is measurable or non-measurable. Non-measurable data, also called unknown and unknowable data,[6] frequently include the most important business figures, such as the cost of an unhappy customer or the benefits of a prideful employee. It is not accurate to assume that if a process cannot be measured, it cannot be managed. Non-measurable data, like interactions with other people, are managed on an ongoing basis.

---

6. The notion of unknown and unknowable control items is taken from Deming, W.E., *Out of the Crisis,* MIT Center for Advanced Engineering Studies (Cambridge, MA), 1986, pp. 121-122.

Integrated Flowchart Showing
Value Added and Non-Values Added Steps

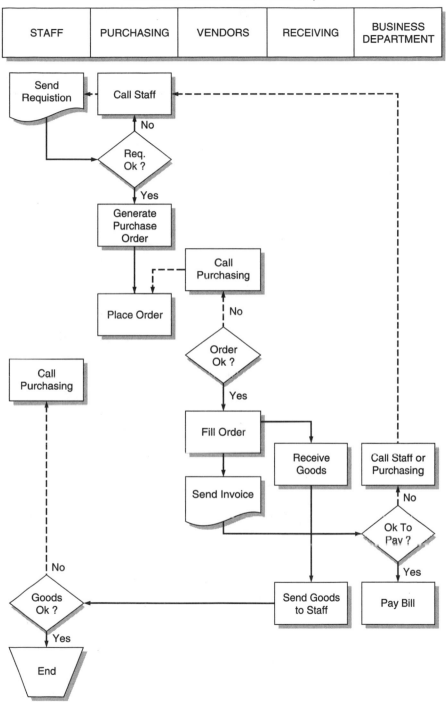

Figure 4.2
Adapted from PQ Systems, Inc., *Total Quality Transformation*, (Miamisburg, OH), undated.

The Do stage entails a project team conducting a planned experiment to determine the optimal configuration of the "best practice method" on a trial basis, as monitored through measurements. The Study stage consists of project team members studying the effectiveness of the "best practice." The Act stage involves the establishment of a standardized best practice method, using a best practice flowchart. This is then formalized by training all relevant employees in the best practice method and by updating training manuals.

A best practice method can be quite complex. It can be constructed to take into account a great number of contingencies. For example, if a customer has complaint A, follow method A; however, if a customer has complaint B, follow method B, and so on. Or, if a customer has complaint A and claims it is urgent, follow method A1; however, if a customer has complaint A and places no urgency on the matter, follow method A2.

Measurements

Best practice methods are monitored through measurements. Measurements possess two important characteristics that make them useful in a system of quality management. First, they are operationally defined. They have a uniformly agreed upon definition[7] which promotes communication between

---

7. Gitlow, H., Oppenheim, A., and Oppenheim, R., *Quality Management: Tools and Methods for Improvement,* 2nd ed., Richard D. Irwin (Homewood, IL), 1995.

people. Second, they monitor "results" and the "processes that generate results."

Measurements are either results-oriented or process-oriented. Results-oriented measurements, called R criteria, are used to evaluate the results of a method. They are called control points (also check points). Process-oriented measurements, called P criteria, are used to evaluate a method that creates results. They are called control items (also check items). "P criteria call for a long-term outlook, since they are directed at people's efforts and often require behavioral change. On the other hand, R criteria are more direct and short term."[8] Figure 4.3 depicts the relationship between P criteria and R criteria.

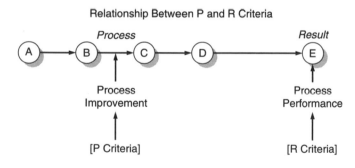

Relationship Between P and R Criteria

Figure 4.3
Modified from Imai, Massaki, *Kaizen: The Key to Japan's Competitive Success*, Random House Business Division (New York, NY), 1st ed., 1986, p. 18

8. Imai, Masaaki, *KAIZEN: The Key to Japan's Competitive Success*, Random House Business Division (New York, NY), 1st ed., 1986, p. 18.

The relationship between control points and control items is shown in the following example. Safety is a control item (P criteria), while the number of injuries per 100 employees per month is a control point (R criteria).

The relationship between manager and subordinate can be defined in terms of control items and control points. A control item for a manager (e.g., safety) is measured or evaluated at a control point by a subordinate (e.g., number of injuries per 100 employees per month). In this way, an interlocking set of R and P measurements are developed throughout an organization.

Daily Management

After a best practice method has been developed and deployed by a project team, housekeeping activities give way to daily management activities. Daily management is used to determine the actions necessary for a project team to maintain, improve, or innovate methods. Daily management is performed to decrease the difference between process (actual) performance and customer requirements. A process with a large variance not centered on a desired customer requirement creates a problematic difference between process performance and customer needs. Daily management is needed to reduce process variation and center the process on the nominal (the desired customer requirement).

Daily management is accomplished by using the PDSA cycle. The PDSA cycle[9] consists of four stages: "PLAN," "DO,"
"STUDY," and "ACT." A Plan is developed
to improve or innovate a standardized
"best practice" method (Plan). A plan can
take the form of a modified "best practice"
flowchart. Ideas for improvement or innovation of a flowchart come from study of
the causal factors that affect a process.
There are many tools that can be used to
help employees understand causal factors,
some of which were mentioned earlier in
the section on the SDSA cycle of housekeeping. The Plan is monitored by taking measurements on a small-scale or trial basis,
and tested through a planned experiment
by project team members (Do). The effects
of the Plan are studied (Study), and appropriate corrective actions are taken (Act).
These corrective actions can lead to a new
or modified Plan, or are formalized through
training all relevant employees and updating training manuals. The PDSA cycle continues forever in an uphill progression of
never-ending improvement.

It is important to note that the success of another person or organization is not a rational basis for turning the PDSA cycle. For example, isolating one component of System
A and expecting it to work within the context of System B is not rational. The reasons

---

9. Deming, W. E., *Out of the Crisis*, MIT CAES, Cambridge,
    MA (1986), pp. 86-89.

behind the success in System A may not be present in System B. Therefore, copying, without a true understanding of the conditions (causal factors) surrounding the copied system, can lead to misapplication of the PDSA cycle. For example, an electric utility copying the customer service process from a manufacturing company, without understanding the reasons why the customer service process was successful in the manufacturing company, can lead to a poorly conceived revised best practice method for the electric utility and, hence, a misapplication of the PDSA cycle.

Personal Example
of Daily Management

Bart's exercise regimen is important to him. He realizes that he is not exercising as much as he would like. He collects data on his exercise habits for a period of eight weeks. The data from his initial investigation is shown in Figure 4.4.

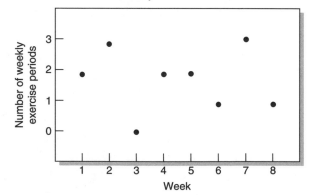

Figure 4.4

Analysis of the data leads Bart to question his method for "making exercise happen." He realizes that he has no method, so he develops the flowchart shown in Figure 4.5.

Flowchart of Exercise Program

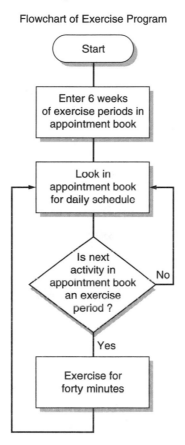

Figure 4.5

Bart discusses his exercise method with his physician during week 9 of his exercise process. His physician states, based on medical knowledge, that Bart should exercise for 40 minutes, at least three times per week. Thus, he establishes a target of three exer-

95

cise periods per week. The measurement for this method is the number of 40-minute exercise periods per week. Bart records the number of 40-minute exercise period per week. The record is shown in Figure 4.6.

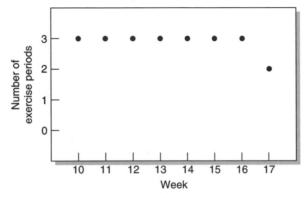

Figure 4.6

The record shows that the target of three exercise periods per week is achieved for weeks 10 through 16, but not in week 17. This leads Bart to go back and examine his method. In so doing, he discovers that the reason he failed to exercise three times in week 17 was that he had no notation for exercise in his appointment book in week 17. He realizes that his exercise method has to be changed to prevent this problem from happening in the future. He revises his method to add in a notation to "write in more exercise periods" after his last noted exercise period. This revision to his method is shown in Figure 4.7.

Revised Flowchart of Exercise Program

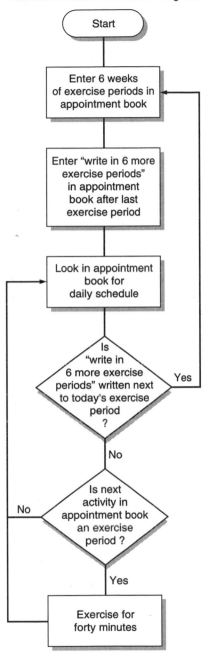

Figure 4.7

Bart collected more data and consistently met his target for weeks 18 through 25; see Figure 4.8.

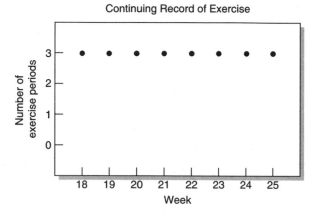

Figure 4.8

Management Review   Project teams present their housekeeping and daily management projects to managers for approval in management reviews. A management review[10] involves comparing the actual results generated by applying a set of methods with the targets established to allocate resources to optimize the organization toward its aim, and finding opportunities to improve and innovate methods.

Three critical inputs are required for a management review. They are a well-researched method (called a "best" practice method), a target established to allocate resources to optimize the aim of the organization, and an actual result that has been measured through a control point.

---

10. Mizuno, pp. 269-280.

The development of the first and second inputs requires that a manager have a deep and thorough understanding of the method being studied, a firm grasp on where the method stands in respect to process capability and environment, knowledge of the aim of the organization to determine appropriate methods to get there,[11] realization that a method is used to predict a result, recognition that a method should yield a high likelihood of achieving a target before it is implemented,[12] and understanding that targets are vehicles for allocating resources between methods.

A set of suggested questions that can form the basis of a management review of a project team is listed below. These questions will help all stakeholders involved in a management review focus on opportunities for improvement and innovation of methods. These questions are only suggestions. Management reviews have natural flows. A manager can use preset questions, but also needs to go with the rhythm of the review if he or she is to accomplish the purpose of the review.

1. What is your group's first priority method?

2. Are you (as an individual) or your group working on improvement or innovation of your first priority method?

---

11. Mizuno, p. 98.
12. Adapted from Mizuno, p. 99.

3. How do you measure the performance of the first priority method? What are the control items and control points for this method?

4. What is your group's target for this method? Monthly? Yearly?

5. Did you study this method last year? How have you incorporated the results of that study into your current method?

6. What is the status of your group's method to date?

7. Are methods yielding targets? Monthly? Yearly?

8. If targets are not being achieved, what countermeasures have your team members taken, and what actions will prevent the same situation from recurring in the future?

A management review probes the root cause(s) of the differences between actual results and targets without "tampering" with methods.

A management review includes a questioning process that asks questions "one inch wide and one mile deep," as opposed to questions which are "one mile wide and one inch deep." This means that the management review probes root causes to a level of detail almost unheard of in the Western world. A technique that helps people probe for root causes in the above manner is the "5W1H" process.[13] The "5W1H" process is used to ask

---

13. Imai Massaki., *Kaizen:The Key to Japan's Success*, Random House Business Division (New York, NY), 1986, p. 235.

"Why" a problem occurs five times and then "How" the problem can be resolved, as opposed to just asking "How" the problem can be resolved. Historically, in the Western world, a person asks a question like, "Why didn't the lawn get mowed this week?" and gets an answer like, "The mower broke." This usually leads to the person responsible for mowing the lawn being blamed and no improvement of the lawn-mowing process. What the "5W1H" process is suggesting is something like the following:

Sample "5W1H" Process

Question 1: "*Why* didn't the lawn get mowed this week?"

Answer 1: "The mower broke."

Question 2: "*Why* did the mower break?"

Answer 2: "The bearing burned out."

Question 3: "*Why* did the bearing burn out?"

Answer 3: "The bearing burned out because it wasn't oiled properly."

Question 4: "*Why* wasn't the bearing oiled properly?"

Answer 4: "The bearing wasn't oiled properly because the oil line was clogged."

Question 5: "*Why* was the oil line clogged?"

Sample "5W1H" Process (Continued)

Answer 5:   "The oil line was clogged because there is no routine and proactive maintenance program to examine the oil line."

Question 6:   *"How* can we resolve this problem so it doesn't happen again?"

Answer 6:   "Develop and follow a policy of routine and proactive maintenance for the oil line."

As you can see, questions one through five focus on the root cause ("Why") of the problem, while the last question focuses on "How" to improve a process. The above example is an application of the "5W1H" process. The "5" and "1" are just symbolic numbers, which promote asking questions that are "one inch wide and one mile deep."

Variance Analysis

It is critical that management reviews be conducted in accordance with Dr. Deming's theory of management. All sources of variation are not due to special causes. A manager following Dr. Deming's theory of management doesn't tamper with the processes under his or her control. Instead, causes of variation are separated into common and special sources by statistical methods. Then employees work to resolve special sources of variation, and management works to remove common sources of variation by modifying methods.

The management review focuses on whether the actual method (the method actually used by an employee) followed the best practice method. Figure 4.9[14] shows the relationship between following methods and achieving targets.

Relationships Between Following Methods
and Achieving Targets

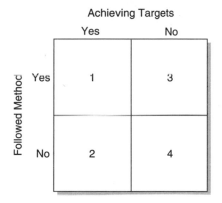

Figure 4.9

Cell 1 shows the outcome of an employee following a best practice method as the attainment of a target.

Cell 4 shows the outcome of an employee not following a best practice method as the failure to attain a target. To reverse this failure, the employee follows the best practice method. In this case, the management review determines answers to the following questions:

---

14. The matrix was discussed by Dr. Noriaki Kano on April 1, 1990 in Atlanta, GA.

1. What best practice method was not followed?

2. Who failed to follow the best practice method? Note: The focus is on system problems, not on the individual. This will promote joy in work and pride in the outcome.

3. Why didn't the employee follow the best practice method? Was it due to ignorance, misunderstanding, lack of training, negligence, problems with a machine, or problems with raw materials?

4. Should the best practice method be changed to resolve problems due to ignorance, misunderstanding, lack of training, negligence, problems with a machine, or problems with raw materials?

Cell 2 shows the outcome of an employee not following a best practice method as the attainment of a target. In this case, depending on prevailing pressures, the employee may adopt a slower pace when determining why the method used yielded the target.

Cell 3 shows the outcome of an employee following the best practice method as the failure to attain a target. In this case, the best practice method is improved or innovated, and/or a change is made in the target; the employee is not blamed. This change is accomplished by asking the following questions:[15]

---

15. The information in this paragraph is adapted from comments made by Dr. Noriaki Kano, Science University of Tokyo, on April 1, 1990, in Atlanta, GA.

1. What best practice method missed its target?

2. How can the best practice method be changed to attain its target?

3. Must the best practice method be changed to resolve problems due to ignorance, misunderstanding, lack of training, problems with a machine, or problems with raw materials?

4. What target was missed?

5. How much was the target missed over time? Is the process under study stable? Will adjustment of the target result in tampering with the best practice method?

6. Why was the target missed? Was the target set incorrectly due to ignorance, lack of training, problems with a machine, problems with raw materials, management or by guesswork?

Once these questions are answered, the necessary information may be available for improvement or innovation of the best practice method or change of the target. These questions focus on improvement and innovation of the best practice method, not on blame of the individual.

Frequently, it is not possible to investigate the negative scenario presented in cell 3 on a daily basis. One day may not provide enough time to perform all four stages of the PDSA cycle to achieve the desired improvement and/or innovation. A special procedure called the Quality Improvement (QI) story is needed to deal with pressing daily problems.

QI Story

The Quality Improvement (QI) story[16] is an efficient format for presenting process improvement studies to management. QI stories standardize the reporting of process improvement efforts, help avoid logical errors in analysis, and make process improvement efforts easier to deploy company-wide. QI stories also promote management based on data and facts, as opposed to management based on guesswork and opinion.

The QI story has seven steps (see Figure 4.10). All sections of a QI story are clearly numbered and labeled so that they can be related to one of the steps in a QI story.

This seven-step procedure follows the PDSA cycle. The PLAN phase involves selecting a theme for the QI story, based on all the background information necessary for understanding the selected theme, including a process flow diagram, the reason for selecting the theme, and organization and department objective(s); gaining a full understanding of the present situation surrounding the theme; and conducting an

16. Gitlow, H., Gitlow, S., Oppenheim, A., and Oppenheim, R., "Telling the Quality Story," *Quality Progress*, September 1990, pp. 41-46.

Relationship between the QI Story and the PDSA Cycle

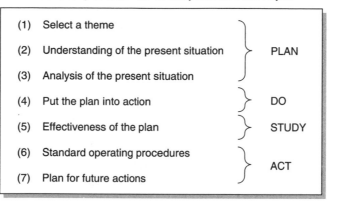

(1) Select a theme

(2) Understanding of the present situation } PLAN

(3) Analysis of the present situation

(4) Put the plan into action } DO

(5) Effectiveness of the plan } STUDY

(6) Standard operating procedures

(7) Plan for future actions } ACT

Figure 4.10
Slightly modified from Imai, Massaki, *Kaizen—The Keys to Japan's Competitive success*, Random House Business Division, NY, 1986, p. 76.

analysis of the present situation to construct a plan of action.

The DO phase involves putting the appropriate plan into action on a small-scale or trial basis so that the process improvement actions can be tested through a designed experiment.

The STUDY phase involves studying, creatively thinking about, collecting, and analyzing data concerning the effectiveness of the plan experimentally set into motion in the Do phase. Does the plan reduce the difference between customer needs and process performance? Before-and-after comparisons of the effects of the experimental plan are presented in a QI story.

Finally, the ACT phase involves determining if the plan was effective in reducing the difference between process performance and customer needs. If it was not effective, employees go back to the PLAN stage to find other actions. If it was effective, employees either go to the PLAN stage to seek the optimal settings of the actions or formally establish revised "best practice" methods through training and updating training manuals. Further actions are taken to prevent backsliding for the plan set into motion. This step also includes identifying remaining process problems, establishing a plan for further actions, and reflecting on the positive and negative aspects of past actions.

Potential Difficulties

When using QI stories, difficulties may arise in two areas: qualitative (non-numerical) themes and exogenous problems. Qualitative themes are QI story themes that are difficult to describe with numerical values. For example, a qualitative theme for a QI story is "Improvement of Management Reviews." Qualitative themes are analyzed by focusing on the magnitude of the gap between actual performance and desired performance. Furthermore, they are improved based on decisions that stem from a manager's theory of management, not from data analysis. For example, the decision to improve the management review process is made on the basis of theory because no data exists on the negative effects of a suboptimal management review process.

Exogenous problems are problems that are seemingly beyond the control of anyone in the organization (e.g., electrical outages caused by power lines being knocked out due to lightning). It is important for employees to realize that it may be possible to take actions to remedy exogenous problems, as opposed to becoming overwhelmed and frustrated by them. When exogenous problems occur, employees analyze why there are so many occurrences of the exogenous problem in area A versus area B, given both areas have equal opportunities for the occurrence of the exogenous problem. This may lead to the isolation of an action that decreases the difference between process performance and customer needs.

For years it was believed that electrical outages due to lightning striking power lines was an exogenous problem at Florida Power & Light Company. A QI story revealed that the incidence of outages in FP&L's South Dade district was much higher than in their West Broward district. Further study showed that the methods used for grounding power lines were different in both areas. This analysis led to the South Dade district's adopting the West Broward district's method for grounding power lines. Subsequently, the incidence of outages due to lightning dropped dramatically in the South Dade district. This seemingly exogenous problem was improved by the application of a QI story.

Pursuit of Objectives

Initially, QI stories will be selected because they are near-complete resolutions to department problems and will not relate to organization and department objectives. As employees gain experience with QI stories, they will want to select themes that do relate to organization and department objectives. If QI story activities are not consistent with department objectives, and department objectives are not consistent with organization objectives, there is the distinct possibility that quality improvement efforts will not be in line with organization goals.

QI Story Case Study

A QI story drawn from a data processing department is presented to demonstrate the role of QI stories in an organization's improvement efforts.[17] The QI story is presented in Figure 4.11.

This QI story goes through two iterations of the PDSA cycle; however, a never-ending set of PDSA iterations will follow as the data processing department pursues continuous improvement in its daily work. The first iteration of the PDSA cycle focuses attention on all data entry operators in the data processing department. In this iteration of the PDSA cycle, selecting a theme is presented in QI story board 1. This includes showing the background of theme selection and the reason for selecting the theme in relation to the organization's and department's objectives. An understanding of the present situation is presented in QI story

17. See Gitlow, H., Oppenheim, A., and Oppenheim, R.,
    Quality Management: Tools and Methods for Improvement,
    2nd ed., Richard D. Irwin, Inc. (Homewood, IL), 1995.

QI STORY BOARD 1

Source: Gitlow, Oppenheim and Oppenheim, *Quality Management: Tools and Methods for Improvement,* Richard D. Irwin, Inc. (Homewood, IL), Second edition, 1994.

Figure 4.11
Quality Improvement Story *(Page 1 of 16)*

111

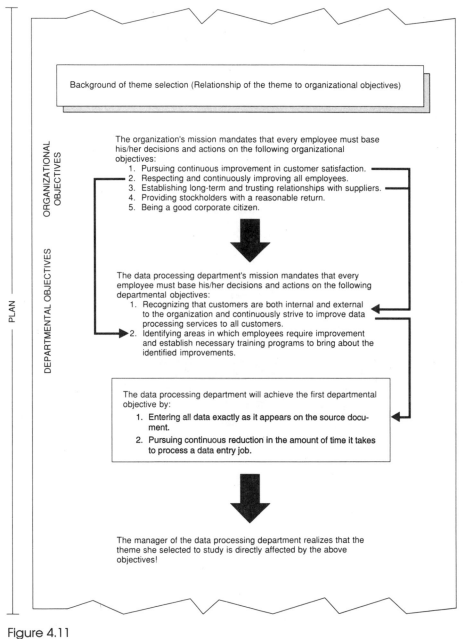

Figure 4.11
Quality Improvement Story *(Page 2 of 16)*

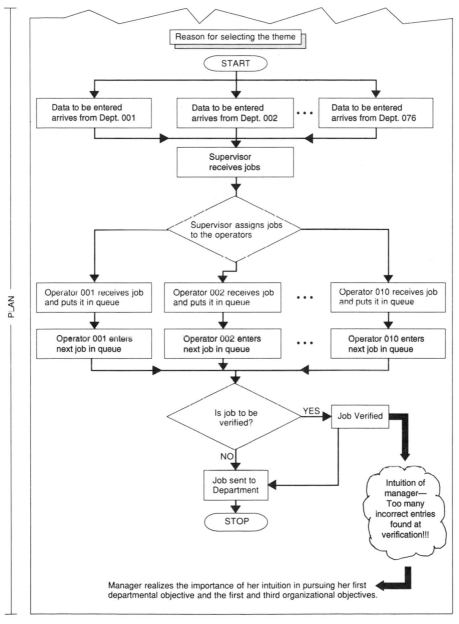

Figure 4.11
Quality Improvement Story *(Page 3 of 16)*

QI STORY BOARD 2

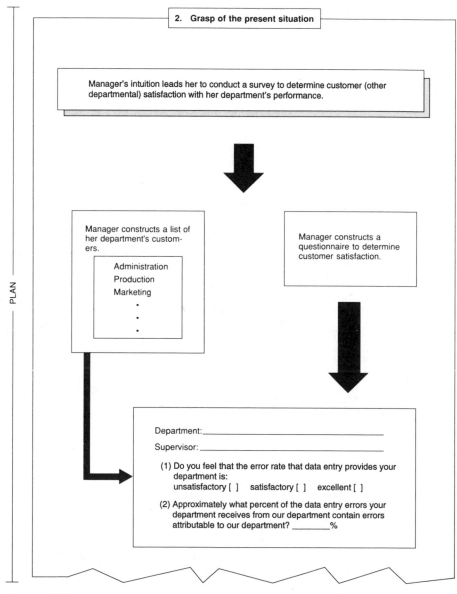

2. Grasp of the present situation

Manager's intuition leads her to conduct a survey to determine customer (other departmental) satisfaction with her department's performance.

Manager constructs a list of her department's customers.

Administration
Production
Marketing
.
.
.

Manager constructs a questionnaire to determine customer satisfaction.

PLAN

Department:_____

Supervisor: _____

(1) Do you feel that the error rate that data entry provides your department is:
unsatisfactory [ ]   satisfactory [ ]   excellent [ ]

(2) Approximately what percent of the data entry errors your department receives from our department contain errors attributable to our department? _____%

Figure 4.11
Quality Improvement Story *(Page 4 of 16)*

114

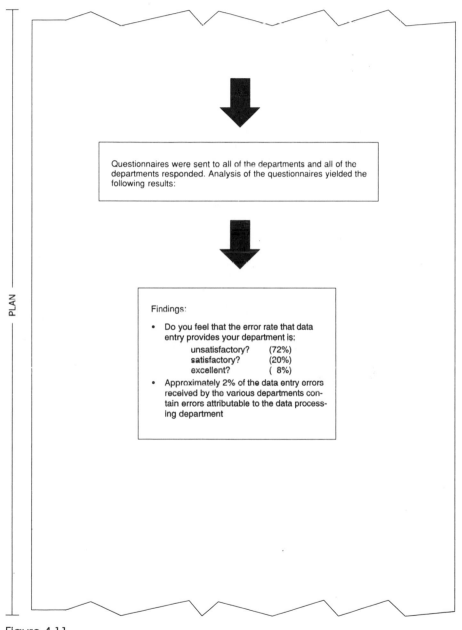

PLAN

Questionnaires were sent to all of the departments and all of the departments responded. Analysis of the questionnaires yielded the following results:

Findings:

- Do you feel that the error rate that data entry provides your department is:
    - unsatisfactory?   (72%)
    - satisfactory?   (20%)
    - excellent?   (8%)
- Approximately 2% of the data entry errors received by the various departments contain errors attributable to the data processing department

Figure 4.11
Quality Improvement Story *(Page 5 of 16)*

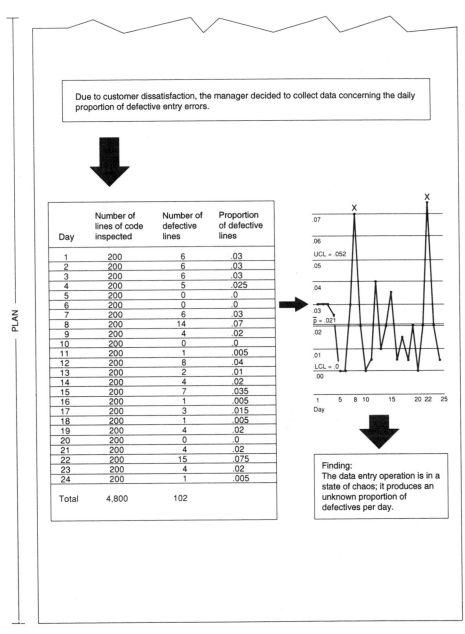

Due to customer dissatisfaction, the manager decided to collect data concerning the daily proportion of defective entry errors.

Day	Number of lines of code inspected	Number of defective lines	Proportion of defective lines
1	200	6	.03
2	200	6	.03
3	200	6	.03
4	200	5	.025
5	200	0	.0
6	200	0	.0
7	200	6	.03
8	200	14	.07
9	200	4	.02
10	200	0	.0
11	200	1	.005
12	200	8	.04
13	200	2	.01
14	200	4	.02
15	200	7	.035
16	200	1	.005
17	200	3	.015
18	200	1	.005
19	200	4	.02
20	200	0	.0
21	200	4	.02
22	200	15	.075
23	200	4	.02
24	200	1	.005
Total	4,800	102	

PLAN

Finding:
The data entry operation is in a state of chaos; it produces an unknown proportion of defectives per day.

Figure 4.11
Quality Improvement Story *(Page 6 of 16)*

QI STORY BOARD 3

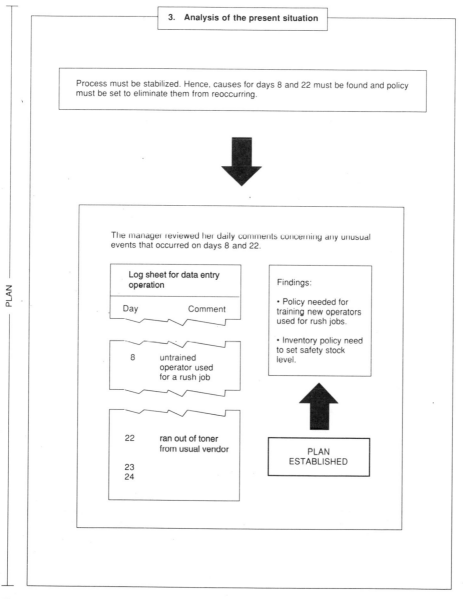

3. Analysis of the present situation

PLAN

Process must be stabilized. Hence, causes for days 8 and 22 must be found and policy must be set to eliminate them from reoccurring.

The manager reviewed her daily comments concerning any unusual events that occurred on days 8 and 22.

Log sheet for data entry operation

Day	Comment
8	untrained operator used for a rush job
22	ran out of toner from usual vendor
23	
24	

Findings:

• Policy needed for training new operators used for rush jobs.

• Inventory policy need to set safety stock level.

PLAN ESTABLISHED

Figure 4.11
Quality Improvement Story *(Page 7 of 16)*

117

QI STORY BOARD 4

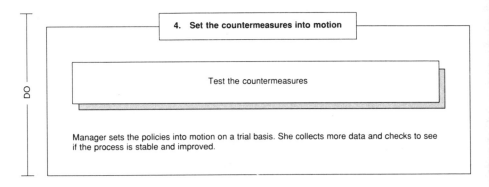

4. Set the countermeasures into motion

Test the countermeasures

Manager sets the policies into motion on a trial basis. She collects more data and checks to see if the process is stable and improved.

QI STORY BOARD 5

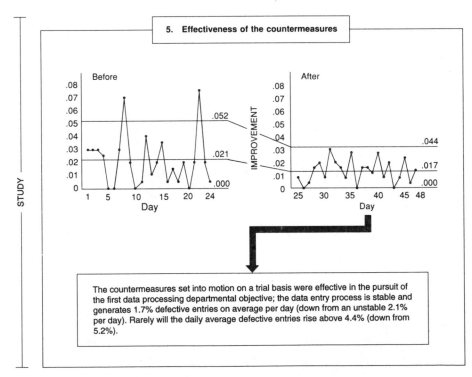

5. Effectiveness of the countermeasures

The countermeasures set into motion on a trial basis were effective in the pursuit of the first data processing departmental objective; the data entry process is stable and generates 1.7% defective entries on average per day (down from an unstable 2.1% per day). Rarely will the daily average defective entries rise above 4.4% (down from 5.2%).

Figure 4.11
Quality Improvement Story *(Page 8 of 16)*

QI STORY BOARD 6

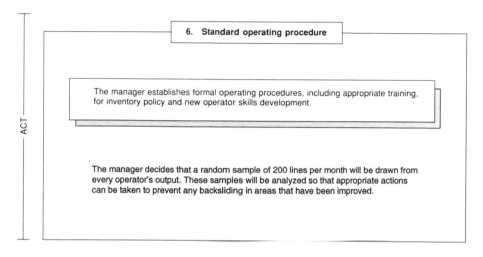

6. Standard operating procedure

The manager establishes formal operating procedures, including appropriate training, for inventory policy and new operator skills development.

The manager decides that a random sample of 200 lines per month will be drawn from every operator's output. These samples will be analyzed so that appropriate actions can be taken to prevent any backsliding in areas that have been improved.

ACT

QI STORY BOARD 7

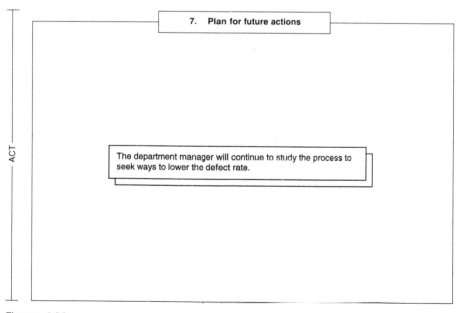

7. Plan for future actions

The department manager will continue to study the process to seek ways to lower the defect rate.

ACT

Figure 4.11
Quality Improvement Story *(Page 9 of 16)*

QI STORY BOARD 8

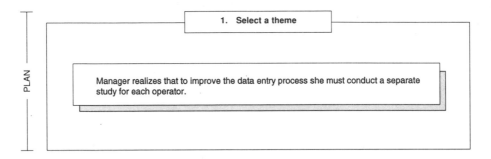

PLAN

1. Select a theme

Manager realizes that to improve the data entry process she must conduct a separate study for each operator.

QI STORY BOARD 9

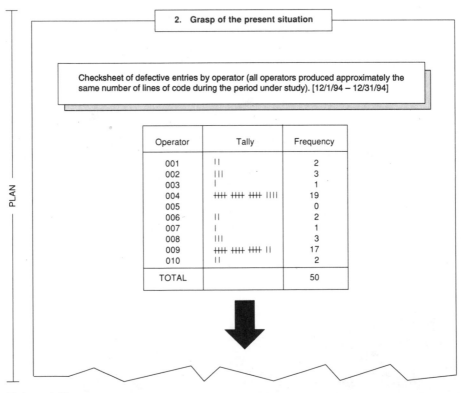

PLAN

2. Grasp of the present situation

Checksheet of defective entries by operator (all operators produced approximately the same number of lines of code during the period under study). [12/1/94 – 12/31/94]

Operator	Tally	Frequency
001	I I	2
002	I I I	3
003	I	1
004	ﬀﬀ ﬀﬀ ﬀﬀ IIII	19
005		0
006	I I	2
007	I	1
008	I I I	3
009	ﬀﬀ ﬀﬀ ﬀﬀ II	17
010	I I	2
TOTAL		50

Figure 4.11
Quality Improvement Story *(Page 10 of 16)*

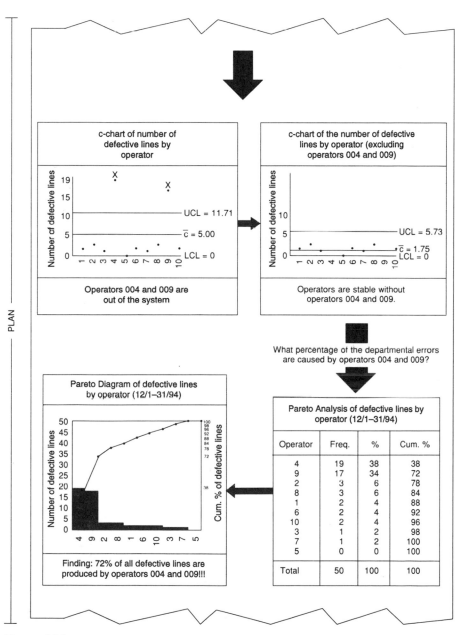

Figure 4.11
Quality Improvement Story *(Page 11 of 16)*

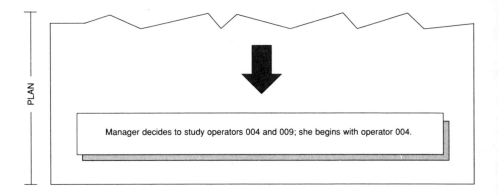

Manager decides to study operators 004 and 009; she begins with operator 004.

QI STORY BOARD 10

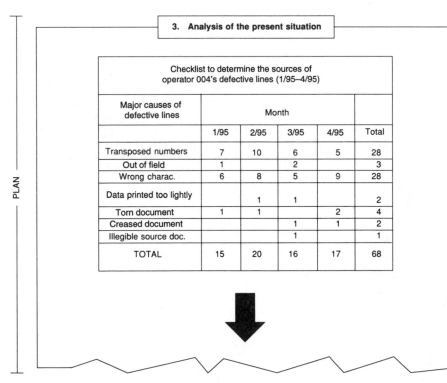

3. Analysis of the present situation

Checklist to determine the sources of
operator 004's defective lines (1/95–4/95)

Major causes of defective lines	Month				
	1/95	2/95	3/95	4/95	Total
Transposed numbers	7	10	6	5	28
Out of field	1		2		3
Wrong charac.	6	8	5	9	28
Data printed too lightly		1	1		2
Torn document	1	1		2	4
Creased document			1	1	2
Illegible source doc.			1		1
TOTAL	15	20	16	17	68

Figure 4.11
Quality Improvement Story *(Page 12 of 16)*

PLAN

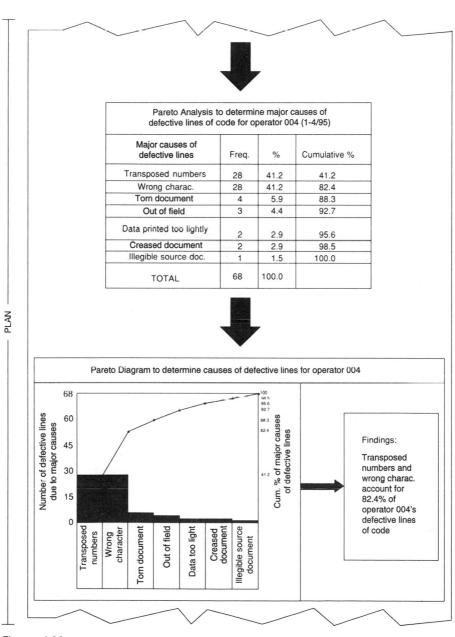

Figure 4.11
Quality Improvement Story *(Page 13 of 16)*

123

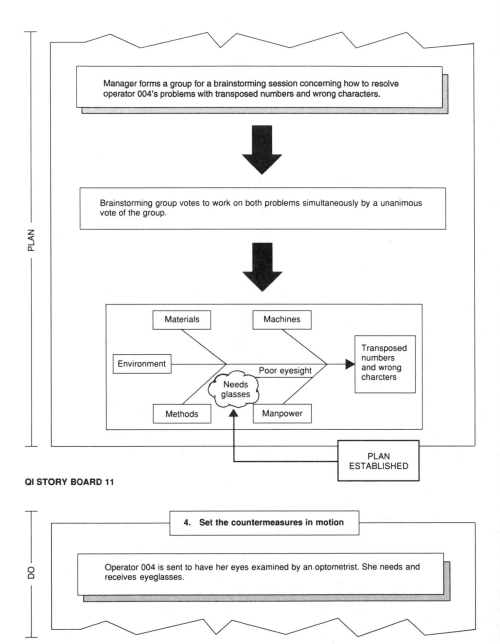

PLAN

Manager forms a group for a brainstorming session concerning how to resolve operator 004's problems with transposed numbers and wrong characters.

Brainstorming group votes to work on both problems simultaneously by a unanimous vote of the group.

Materials

Machines

Environment

Poor eyesight

Needs glasses

Methods

Manpower

Transposed numbers and wrong charcters

PLAN ESTABLISHED

QI STORY BOARD 11

4. Set the countermeasures in motion

DO

Operator 004 is sent to have her eyes examined by an optometrist. She needs and receives eyeglasses.

Figure 4.11
Quality Improvement Story *(Page 14 of 16)*

QI STORY BOARD 12

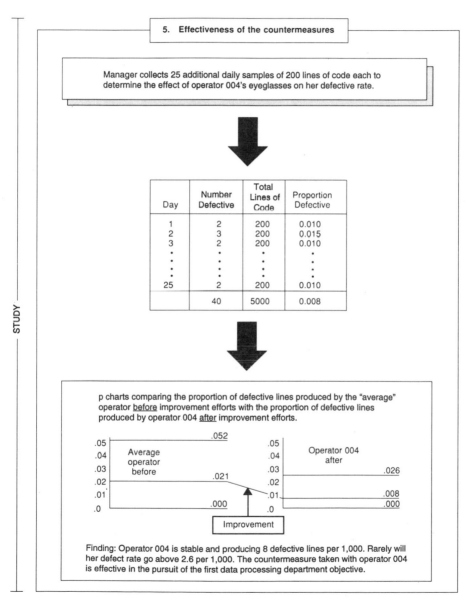

Figure 4.11
Quality Improvement Story *(Page 15 of 16)*

QI STORY BOARD 13

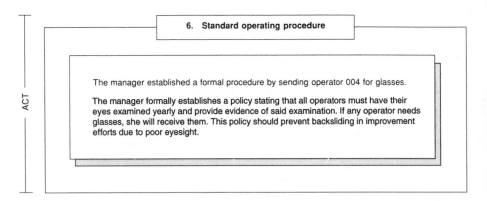

6. **Standard operating procedure**

ACT

The manager established a formal procedure by sending operator 004 for glasses.

The manager formally establishes a policy stating that all operators must have their eyes examined yearly and provide evidence of said examination. If any operator needs glasses, she will receive them. This policy should prevent backsliding in improvement efforts due to poor eyesight.

QI STORY BOARD 14

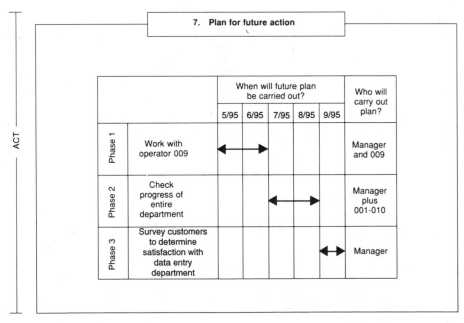

7. **Plan for future action**

		When will future plan be carried out?					Who will carry out plan?
		5/95	6/95	7/95	8/95	9/95	
Phase 1	Work with operator 009	◄──►					Manager and 009
Phase 2	Check progress of entire department			◄──►			Manager plus 001-010
Phase 3	Survey customers to determine satisfaction with data entry department					◄─►	Manager

Figure 4.11
Quality Improvement Story *(Page 16 of 16)*

126

board 2. An analysis of the present situation, which is shown in QI story board 3, is performed to determine an appropriate plan that pursues the theme and the organization and department objectives. Setting the plan into motion on a trial basis is presented in QI story board 4. The effectiveness of the plan, on the theme and the organization and department objectives, is measured. This is shown in QI story board 5. Standard operating procedure is set, which formalizes the countermeasures and prevents backsliding. This is shown in QI story board 6. A plan for future actions is in QI story board 7.

The second iteration of the PDSA cycle focuses attention on an individual data entry operator. In this iteration, selecting a theme is accomplished when the data processing manager realizes that future process improvements require her to identify and train operators whose performance is out of control on the low side (see QI story board 8). An understanding of the present situation determined that data entry operators 004 and 009 were out of control on the high side. This is presented in QI story board 9. An analysis of the present situation, which is shown in QI story board 10, determined the actions necessary to improve operator 004. The manager put the plan into action. This is shown in QI story board 11. The positive effect of the plan on operator 004 and the organization and department objective was confirmed (see QI story board 12). Standard operating procedure was set and formalized the actions of all operators to prevent backsliding. This is presented in QI story board 13. Finally, a plan for future actions is specified in QI story board 14.

Empowerment

Steps 18 and 19 of the Detailed Fork Model include empowering employees through daily management.[18] Empowerment is a term commonly used by managers in today's organizational environment. However, empowerment has not been operationally defined, and its definition varies from application to application. Currently, the popular definition of empowerment relies loosely on the notion of dropping decision-making down to the lowest appropriate level in an organization. The basic premise of empowerment is that if people are given the authority to make decisions, they will take pride in their work, be willing to take risks, and work harder to make things happen. Frequently, the reality of empowerment is that employees are empowered until they make a mistake; then the hatchet falls. Most employees know this and treat the popular concept of empowerment with the lack of respect it merits. Empowerment in its current form is destructive to quality management.

18. The information contained in this section was developed by David Pietenpol (Employers Health Insurance, Green Bay, WI) and Howard Gitlow.

Empowerment in a quality management sense has a dramatically different aim and definition. The aim of empowerment in quality management is to increase pride in work and joy in the outcome for all employees. The definition of empowerment that translates the above aim into a realistic objective follows. Empowerment is a process that provides an individual or group of employees the opportunity to:

1.   Define and document methods

2.   Learn about methods through training and development

3.   Improve and innovate best practice methods that make up systems

4.   Utilize latitude in their own judgement to make decisions within the context of best practice methods

5.   Trust superiors to react positively to the latitude taken by employees making decisions within the context of best practice methods

Empowerment starts with leadership, but requires the commitment of all employees. Leaders provide employees with all five items stated above.

Employees accept responsibility for:

1.   Increasing their training and knowledge of methods and the systems of which they are a part

2.   Participating in the development, standardization, improvement, and innovation of best practice methods

129

3. Increasing their latitude in decision-making within the context of best practice methods

Latitude to make decisions within the context of a best practice method refers to the options an employee has in resolving a problem within the confines of a best practice method, not to modification of the best practice method. Differentiating between the need to change the best practice method and latitude within the context of the best practice method takes place at the operational level.

Empowerment can only exist in an environment of trust which supports planned experimentation concerning ideas to improve and innovate best practice methods. Ideas for improvement and innovation can come from individuals or from the team, but tests of the worthiness of those ideas are conducted through planned experiments under the auspices of the team (the "Do" stage of the PDSA cycle). Anything else will result in chaos because everybody will do his or her own thing.

Individual employees are taught to understand that increased variability in output will result if each employee follows his or her own method. This increased variability will create additional cost and unpredictable customer service. Employees are educated about the need to reach consensus on one "best practice" method.

The "best practice" method will consist of generalized procedures and individualized procedures. Generalized procedures are standardized procedures that all employees follow. Individualized procedures are procedures that afford each worker the opportunity to utilize their individual differences by creating their own standardized procedure. However, the outputs of individualized procedures are standardized across employees. Individualized procedures can be improved through personal efforts. In the beginning of a quality improvement effort, employees and management may not have the knowledge to allow for individualized procedures.

A professor following an approved departmental syllabus for a certain course is an example of an employee using a generalized procedure. When that professor injects his or her own stories, examples, and jokes, he or she is using individual procedures.

Empowerment is operationalized at two levels. First, employees are empowered to develop and document best practice methods using the SDSA cycle. Second, employees are empowered to improve or innovate best practice methods through application of the PDSA cycle.

More on Daily Management

As managers see the results from improved processes, they will want to expand the number of daily management project teams. This should be discouraged in the beginning of a quality management effort.

131

Instead, managers should be asked to direct their existing project teams to continually PDSA the processes already under study. The benefit of this action is ensuring that managers learn how to continuously improve and innovate processes, not how to make one improvement in a process and jump to another process. Management reviews are an excellent vehicle to promote this type of training experience. Reviewers can ask the following question: "Can I see your improvement action memorandum for this process?" The reviewee should be able to show multiple improvement action memoranda, including changes to training programs, for the process they are studying with their project team.

Coordinating Project Teams: Steps 19 and 20

As the initial process improvement teams begin to show positive results, other process improvement teams will be formed by area or department managers in response to localized issues (see step 19 of the Detailed Fork Model).

The initial and other process improvement teams require resources, such as PILs, members to work on projects, training, financial resources, physical space in which to meet, and the direction and guidance of a higher level of management.

As the number of teams increases, a structure to coordinate and manage the teams at the department level is necessary. The structure is called a Local Steering Team (LST) (see step 20 of the Detailed Fork Model). Each department's LST has the responsibility to coordinate daily management projects (see steps 18 and 19 of the Detailed Fork Model).

Summary

Chapter 4 presents a discussion of Prong Two of the fork model that is presented in this book, daily management. Daily management is used to develop, maintain, improve and innovate the methods employed in daily work.

The first phase of implementing daily management involves selecting initial project teams. Process Improvement Leaders are chosen by the EC and trained in "Basic Quality Control Tools" and "Psychology of the Individual and Team." Then the initial projects are determined, and project teams are formed.

After training, each initial project team works on one or more methods using daily management. Daily management includes housekeeping, which is the development, standardization, and deployment of methods required for daily work, and daily management, which is the maintenance, improvement, and innovation of methods for daily work.

Housekeeping functions are developed through function deployment. This is the way employees determine what functions are required to perform each method they use in their daily work. Housekeeping is accomplished by employing the SDSA cycle. The objective is to determine the "best practice method" for each function. Best practice methods are monitored through measurements that are operationally defined and measure results and the processes that generate results.

After a best practice method has been developed and deployed by a project team, daily management activities begin. Daily management is used to reduce process variation and to center the process on the customer's requirements. The PDSA cycle is utilized in daily management in a continuous progression of never-ending improvement. A personal example of using daily management to improve a "best practice method" for exercise habits is presented in this chapter.

Project teams present their housekeeping and daily management projects to managers in management reviews. This is a process that involves comparing the actual results generated with the targets established. Suggested questions that can form the basis of a management review are listed in this chapter. It is critical that management reviews take into account common and special causes of variation. If a management review is done properly, there is no place for tampering with the process or blaming employees for problems out of their control.

A special procedure called the Quality Improvement (QI) story is used to present and deal with pressing daily problems that cannot be adequately handled through regular reviews. QI stories standardize the reporting of process improvement efforts, help avoid logical errors in analysis, and make process improvement efforts easier to deploy company-wide. The seven-step procedure for constructing a QI story is described in this chapter. A QI story drawn from a data processing department is presented to show the role of QI stories in an organization's improvement efforts.

Empowering employees through daily management is discussed in this chapter. The aim of empowerment in a quality management sense is to increase pride in work and joy in the outcome for all employees. It is operationalized at two levels. First, employees are empowered to develop and document best practice methods using the SDSA cycle. Then they are empowered to improve or innovate best practice methods through the application of the PDSA cycle.

As the initial project teams begin to show positive results, and more teams are formed by area or department managers, a structure is needed to coordinate the teams at the departmental level. This is called the Local Steering Team, and it has the responsibility of coordinating daily management projects.

Cross-Functional Management

Prong Three

Background[1]

Cross-Functional Management is critical to the quality management model because it weaves together the vertical (line) functions of management with the horizontal (interdepartmental) functions of management. Professor Kaoru Ishikawa states "in order to be called a fabric, both horizontal and vertical threads need to be woven together, and only when horizontal

---

1. Kungane, Kenji, *Cross-Functional Management: Principles and Practical Applications,* Asian Producitvity Organization (Tokyo, Japan), 1993, pp. 33-36.

Purpose of this Chapter

The purpose of this chapter is to explain what is required to develop, standardize, deploy, maintain, improve, and innovate methods that cross areas in an organization. Cross-Functional Management is Prong Three of the quality management model presented in this book (see Figure 5.1).

A Model for the Transformation of an Organization

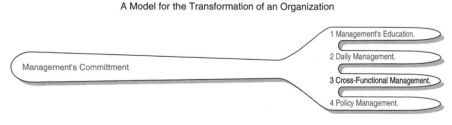

Figure 5.1

threads—or Cross-Functional Management threads—are woven together with vertical threads can a company be considered similarly cohesive."[2] Cross-Functional Management is important because it promotes the reorganization of corporate management systems to improve interdepartmental communication and cooperation, and provides clear lines of responsibility for that reorganization.

The primary areas for the application of Cross-Functional Management include quality management (quality control and quality improvement), cost management (profit management, expense management, and cost reduction), delivery management (production quantity management, delivery date management, and production system management), and personnel management (human development, education, and work morale enhancement). The auxiliary areas for the application of Cross-Functional Management include new product development (R and D, technology development, and production technology), sales management (marketing, sales activity management, and sales expansion), safety management (safety/hygiene control, labor safety control, and environmental control), and QC promotional support (QC circle standardization). Primary cross-functional areas are permanent; however, auxiliary cross-functional areas

2. Kaoru, Ishikawa, "Management in Vertical-Threaded Society," *Quality Control,* vol. 32, no. 1 (1981), pp. 4-5.

change according to current and expected conditions.

Selecting Initial Cross-Functional Teams: Steps 21 Through 24

The members of the EC form initial cross-functional teams (see step 21 of the Detailed Fork Model). The EC selects a leader for each team (see step 22 of the Detailed Fork Model) and allocates appropriate resources for the education and training of the leader (see step 23 of the Detailed Fork Model). Each cross-functional leader is an executive with the title of Senior Vice President or Vice President in charge of a function. The EC uses the recommendations of the team leader to select members for the initial cross-functional teams (see step 24 of the Detailed Fork Model). Team size is kept to a minimum, about five people. All team members are trained in appropriate theory and practice (see step 24 of the Detailed Fork Model). Team members should be executives with the rank of director or above. All team members do not have to come from affected areas. A diversity of opinion and knowledge is helpful, but it is not necessary to have all affected areas represented on a cross-functional team. The team facilitator is an executive in charge of a function, such as personnel. The support staff for a cross-functional team is from the facilitator's home department because the facilitator needs to have the authority to make things happen for his or her cross-functional team.[3]

Doing Cross-Functional Management: Step 25

Cross-Functional Management includes the following activities:

1. Studying and applying Dr. Deming's theory of management and process knowledge to develop, standardize, control, improve, and innovate company-wide systems

2. Developing measurements for company-wide systems

3. Coordinating and optimizing company-wide systems within departmental methods

4. Allocating resources for cross-functional and departmental methods by establishing targets

5. Ensuring that each department performs its deployed methods in daily management

6. Monitoring company-wide systems in respect to targets from a corporate level (management review)

7. If necessary, taking action utilizing the PDSA cycle to decrease the difference between actual results and targets (variance analysis)

---

3. Kurogane, Kenji, *Cross-Functional Management: Principles and Practical Applications*, Asian Productivity Organization (Tokyo, Japan), 1993, p 45.

Finally, as expertise is developed with company-wide systems, it is deployed into daily management methods where appropriate (see step 25 of the Detailed Fork Model).

Several administrative structures can be used to promote Cross-Functional Management. In small organizations, one cross-functional team comprising all relevant executives can be established to coordinate and optimize company-wide systems. In large organizations, one cross-functional team comprising appropriate executives can be established to coordinate and optimize each company-wide system. For example, there could be one team for quality management, one team for safety/hygiene management, and so on. Another alternative for large organizations is to allow a functional department to coordinate and optimize one company-wide system. For example, the Personnel Department could coordinate and optimize the company-wide systems dealing with the enhancement of employee morale.

Frequently, executives claim that they do not have time for Cross-Functional Management due to the demands of their daily routine. It is necessary for these executives to do daily management to remove non-value-added daily routine from their schedules to free up time for Cross-Functional Management.

Cross-functional teams report directly to the members of the EC and have the highest level of decision-making authority. They perform the PLAN and STUDY phases of the PDSA cycle for company-wide systems. Implementation of company-wide systems, the DO and ACT phases of the PDSA cycle, is carried out by line departments in daily management.

Coordinating Cross-Functional Teams: Steps 26 and 27

As the initial cross-functional teams successfully improve company-wide systems, the EC will form new cross-functional teams (see step 26 of the Detailed Fork Model). The EC reviews, manages, and coordinates all cross-functional teams (see step 27 of the Detailed Fork Model).

A Cross-Functional Management review of the line departments affected by cross-functional policy is conducted by a cross-functional team leader. Cross-Functional Management reviews are conducted one or more times per year, study departmental management from a company-wide perspective, and provide feedback to line departments and the cross-functional team for the next year. Line departments report their progress with implementing cross-functional policy by filing a Cross-Functional Management report. The cross-functional team collects all departmental Cross-Functional Management reports and uses them as a basis for conducting reviews and taking action. Furthermore, the Cross-Functional Management team reports their findings to the EC.

Cross-functional teams generate projects that may be sent to the Policy Deployment Committee (see step 29 of the Detailed Fork Model, to be discussed in the next chapter) or a Local Steering Team for action (see step 20 of the Detailed Fork Model).

Some Common Problems Implementing Cross-Functional Management

Cross-functional activities, due to their interdisciplinary structure, are activities that are ripe for misunderstandings between team members, and between team members and the rest of the organization. For example, a cross-functional team working on the budgeting and planning process can easily create confusion, resentment, and fear among the members of an organization. This happens when the cross-functional team changes the methods for allocating resources to departments and thereby reduces a department's ability in the short term to predict its budget line.

Some common mistakes made when cross-functional teams are established are discussed below. The mistakes cover the longevity, membership, focus, resources, and communications of cross-functional teams.

Cross-functional teams are permanent committees that deal with the continuous improvement of important company-wide systems over the long term. Dissolving a cross-functional team after its members have solved some problem in a company-wide system is not advisable. For example, a cross-functional team would be established to improve the company-wide safety/hygiene system over the long term, as opposed to created to deal with a rash of industrial accidents.

Cross-functional teams don't have to include representatives from all areas affected by their policy. Including members from all areas on a cross-functional team may make the team too big to manage well. For example, a cross-functional team that addresses cost management does not have to include representatives from all areas in an organization.

Cross-functional team members transcend the boundaries of their own areas. A person from the production area learns to think in terms of the entire system of interdependent stakeholders when addressing company-wide systems, not from the perspective of the production area. People on cross-functional teams who represent their own special interest groups, not the welfare of the entire organization, are not ready to participate on a cross-functional team. They need further training.

It is extremely important that cross-functional policy be communicated to all relevant members of an organization's interdependent system of stakeholders. Only through communication can people understand and buy into the company-wide changes that can emanate from a cross-functional team.

A Manufacturing Example of Cross-Functional Management: Toyota Forklift

Background

This case study presents an application of Cross-Functional Management in a manufacturing environment. The material in this section was taken from an excellent text by Kenji Kurogane entitled *Cross-Functional Management: Principles and Practical Applications,* Asian Productivity Organization (Tokyo, Japan), 1993, pp. 86-87.[4] The case study presents the background and Quality Assurance model used to promote new product development at Toyota Forklift.

Each division of Toyota is responsible for the development of new products. The process begins with input from the long-range business plan and annual policy statement of a division. The departments in each division responsible for new product development assume development tasks based on Toyota's Quality Assurance system (see Figure

---

4. The material in this case study was rewritten so that it would integrate with the writing style used in this book. The authors take sole responsibility for any errors due to rewriting.

5.2). These departments span product planning through production preparation.

Management reviews are conducted by managers to check and follow up new product development at predetermined intervals. Design reviews are conducted at appropriate places in the Quality Assurance system to determine whether it is appropriate to advance to the next phase of new product development.

Quality Assurance Activity in the Development of the X300 Forklift
Overview

The Toyota design review system was used in the development of the X300 forklift at Toyota Forklift. This system integrated six design reviews into the development of the X300 forklift.

The basic idea behind the development of the X300 forklift was to provide an excellent product through farsighted prediction of market trends and customer needs, and to win customer satisfaction and trust.

Quality Assurance in New Product Development

Quality Improvement in Product Planning. The product planning system used to develop the Toyota Forklift X300 consists of three phases: market research, new product planning, and developing and reviewing the product plan (see Figure 5.3).

The market research phase involves getting a grasp of customer needs and wants by market segment (through surveys) and translating those needs and wants into "demanded quality characteristics" (through Quality Function Deployment).

146

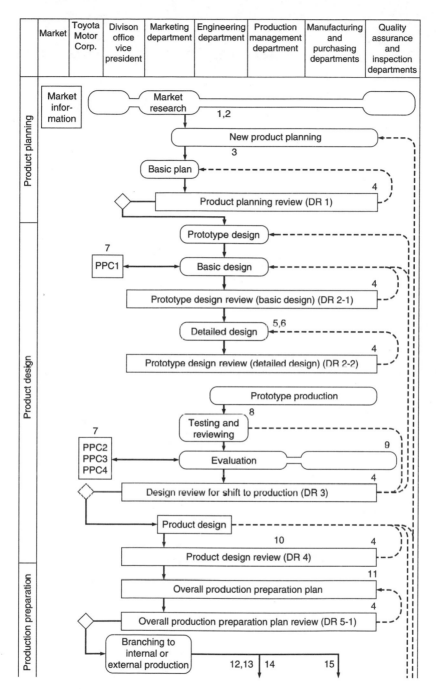

Figure 5.2 *(Page 1 of 2)*
Reprinted from *Cross-Functional Management: Principles and Practical Applications,* Kenji Kurogane, Editor in Chief. Copyright ©1993 by Asian Productivity Organization. Reprinted by permission of the Asian Productivity Organization. Distributed in the U.S., Canada, and Western Europe by Quality Resources, White Plains, NY, 10601.

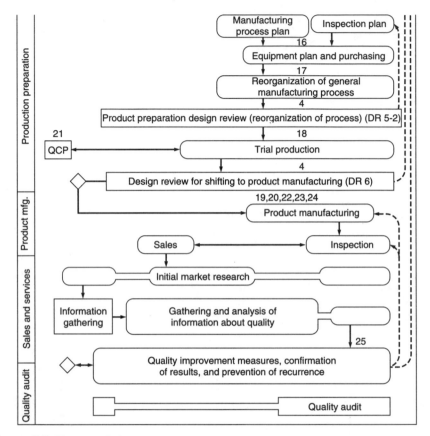

Figure 5.2 *(Page 2 of 2)*
Reprinted from *Cross-Functional Management: Principles and Practical Applications*, Kenji Kurogane, Editor in Chief. Copyright ©1993 by Asian Productivity Organization. Reprinted by permission of the Asian Productivity Organization. Distributed in the U.S., Canada, and Western Europe by Quality Resources, White Plains, NY, 10601.

The new product planning phase involves studying competing products, establishing which "demanded quality characteristics" will stimulate customers to buy in each market segment (called sales points), reviewing the time to market (using Gantt charts, PERT/CPM, or other scheduling

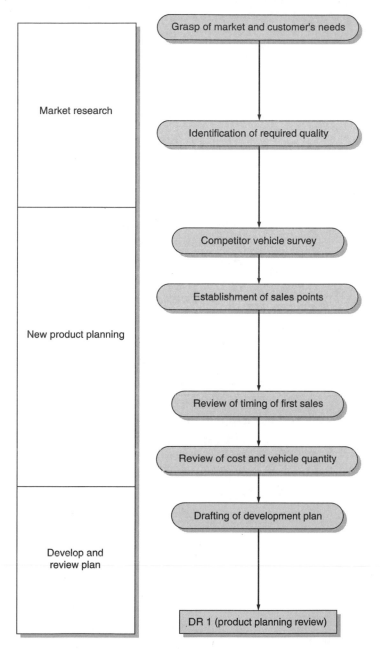

Figure 5.3

Reprinted from *Cross-Functional Management: Principles and Practical Applications,* Kenji Kurogane, Editor in Chief. Copyright ©1993 by Asian Productivity Organization. Reprinted by permission of the Asian Productivity Organization. Distributed in the U.S., Canada, and Western Europe by Quality Resources, White Plains, NY, 10601.

methods), reviewing the production costs of the product, and forecasting the demand for the product in each market segment.

The develop and review plan phase involves drafting a development plan for the X300 Forklift and conducting a product planning review.

Quality Improvement in Product Design. The product design system used to develop the X300 Forklift consists of six phases: prototype design, prototype production, test and review, evaluation, shift to production, and product design (see Figure 5.4).

The prototype design phase involves conducting an "engineering policy review" for the new product functions. This includes developing a detailed list of relevant processes, parts, mechanisms, and functions with specifications (using Quality Function Deployment), preparing a critical functions evaluation report, and performing bottleneck engineering of relevant processes.

The prototype production phase involves a detailed design review of the X300 Forklift.

The test and review and evaluation phases involve establishing test conditions and evaluation criteria through surveys of actual usage conditions and an accelerated endurance bench test. Life expectancy was estimated on the basis of test results and survey data. The above activities increased the degree of comfort at Toyota Forklift in predicting that the design of the X300 was

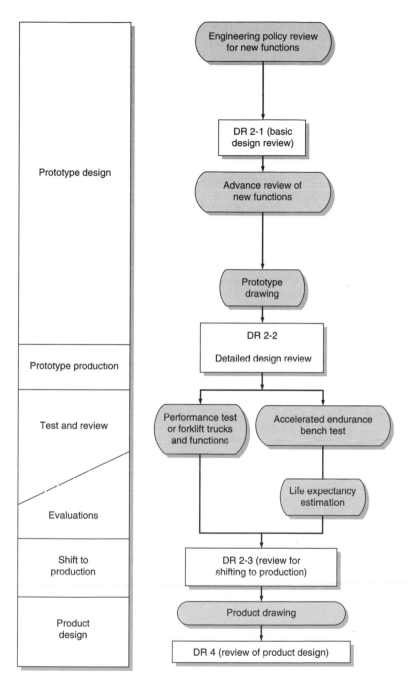

Figure 5.4
Reprinted from *Cross-Functional Management: Principles and Practical Applications,* Kenji Kurogane, Editor in Chief. Copyright ©1993 by Asian Productivity Organization. Reprinted by permission of the Asian Productivity Organization. Distributed in the U.S., Canada, and Western Europe by Quality Resources, White Plains, NY, 10601.

going according to plan and would require few modifications later in its life cycle.

The shift to production phase involves a pass or fail review to shift to trial production.

The product design phase involves the finalization of detailed product drawings and a product design review to determine conformance of design quality to overall quality specifications.

Quality Improvement in Production Preparation. The production preparation system used to develop the X300 Forklift consists of eight phases: developing a general production plan, developing a manufacturing process plan, developing an equipment plan, purchasing equipment, reorganizing individual processes to ensure machine capability, reorganizing the entire production process to ensure system capability, trial production, and shifting to product manufacturing (see Figure 5.5).

The general production plan involves obtaining confirmation of existing product and process problems, conducting a review to determine if those problems have been resolved, and identifying the characteristics of machines and equipment that were deployed in the product design phase through Quality Function Deployment.

The manufacturing process plan involves conducting failure modes and effect analysis (FMEA) on the characteristics of machines and equipment, and discovering any

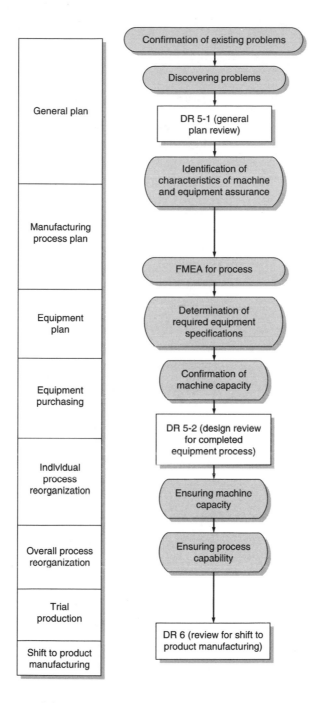

Figure 5.5
Reprinted from *Cross-Functional Management: Principles and Practical Applications,* Kenji Kurogane, Editor in Chief. Copyright ©1993 by Asian Productivity Organization. Reprinted by permission of the Asian Productivity Organization. Distributed in the U.S., Canada, and Western Europe by Quality Resources, White Plains, NY, 10601.

bottleneck problems resulting from equipment and production methods.

The equipment plan phase involves determining the specifications of the equipment required to manufacture the X300 Forklift for cost estimation purposes.

The equipment purchasing phase involves confirming the capability of machines and equipment after specifications have been costed out, generating purchase orders for machinery and equipment, and conducting a design review for the completed machines and equipment processes.

The individual process reorganization phase involves ensuring the capacity of individual machines, and the overall process reorganization phase involves ensuring the capacity of the entire production process. These phases include establishing work procedures, developing operating standards, allocating human resources, developing training programs, and surveying appropriate people to predict the capabilities of machines and the entire system.

The trial production phase and the shift to manufacturing phase involve a pass or fail review of the decision to shift the X300 Forklift to manufacturing.

Concluding Remarks

From the inception of quality management activity at Toyota, top management promoted Cross-Functional Management across divisions to upgrade company-wide systems. As a result, the company successfully solved many problems, promoted standardization of systems, and achieved efficient management. The X300 is a case study in how a cross-functional system was used for new product design.

A Service Example of Cross-Functional Management: Field of Flowers

Background

Field of Flowers is a retailer of flowers and related items located in Davie, Florida. Its President and top management studied Dr. Deming's theory of management and set up the company according to those principles. Field of Flowers is an organization that lives Dr. Deming's theory of management.

When the company was first organized, a performance appraisal system had to be instituted. Since Field of Flowers wanted it to be in keeping with its mission and values, a cross-functional team composed of top managers was organized to develop the system.

The first step for the cross-functional team was to study the theoretical information about performance appraisal in the literature. The following is a summary of the research used by the cross-functional team in their creation of the performance appraisal system.

A company-wide system for performance appraisal includes[5] providing an employee

---

5. The structure of this chapter is heavily drawn from Scholtes, Peter, "An Elaboration on Deming's Teachings on Performance Appraisal," Joiner Associates, Madison, WI, 1987. The authors have modified some of the ideas in Mr. Scholtes' paper and take sole responsibility for their modifications.

155

feedback on his or her work, providing a basis for salary increases and bonuses, identifying candidates for promotion, providing periodic direction of an employee's work, providing an opportunity to give recognition, direction, and feedback to an employee regarding his or her work on special projects, identifying an employee's needs for training, education, and skill or career development, providing an equitable, objective, defensible system that satisfies the requirement of the 1964 Civil Rights Act and the Equal Opportunity Commission guidelines of 1966 and 1970, and providing a channel for communication that otherwise would probably not occur.

Providing an employee feedback on his or her work can be accomplished by identifying the major processes in which the employee is involved, identifying the major work group or groups to which employees belong, developing a list of major feedback resources for each employee (e.g., key customers and suppliers), and developing an agenda and method for obtaining feedback from each feedback resource.

Providing a basis for salary increases and bonuses can be accomplished by basing salaries and bonuses on market rate (what it would cost to replace someone on the open market), accumulation of skills (flexibility due to acquired abilities), accumulation of responsibility (depth of contribution to a greater number of processes and influence over a larger number of employees), seniority within an organization and within a job classification, and prosperity (profit-sharing of the entire organization, not one segment of the organization).

Identifying candidates for promotion can be accomplished by providing special assignments that contain elements of the promotion job to employees, utilizing an assessment center to observe candidates exercising the skills needed in the promotion job under realistic conditions, conducting "voice of the stakeholder" studies to determine the needs and wants of stakeholders in respect to the person who will assume the promotion job, and developing an organizational culture in which promotion is not the only vehicle for people to exercise leadership and influence, to get rewards and recognition, or to stretch and challenge themselves in their jobs and careers.

Providing periodic direction of employees' work can be accomplished by developing and communicating the organization's vision, mission, values, and beliefs, strategic plan, and business plan which guide and define everyone's efforts; spending time with employees planning the methods and targets needed to promote the organization's vision, mission, values, and beliefs, strategic plan, and business plan; and communicating with employees on a daily basis, not tampering with the employees or the processes.

157

Providing an opportunity to give recognition, direction, and feedback to an employee regarding his or her work on special projects can be accomplished by many of the alternatives described above.

Identifying an employee's needs for training, education, and skill or career development can be accomplished by empowering employees (in the quality management sense) and designing methods to determine people's capabilities for each of the competencies necessary for the optimization of the interdependent system of stakeholders.

Providing an equitable, objective, defensible system that satisfies the requirement of the 1964 Civil Rights Act and the Equal Opportunity Commission guidelines of 1966 and 1970 can be accomplished by committing to the values and spirit inscribed in the law, not just by conforming to the law.

Providing a channel for communication that otherwise would probably not occur can be accomplished by all employees in an organization asking and answering the following questions: "With whom is it important to maintain communication? For what purpose? With what frequency? In what kind of setting, format, or agenda?" Answers to the above questions should promote the flow of information and knowledge into channels of communication between people in organizations.

It is important to realize that the above processes form an interdependent system of processes. It does not make sense to adopt a new model for providing employees a basis for salary and bonuses and not provide them a method for identifying needs for training, education, and skill or career development. To do so may create a monster worse than the existing system of performance appraisal. For example, guaranteeing salary based on seniority without any method to improve the employee or organizational processes could be a formula for disaster.

Creating
the Performance
Appraisal System

Once their study was sufficiently advanced, the cross-functional team members worked on their own interpretation and application of the theory. The results of the cross-functional teams's work is presented in the following excerpts, paraphrases, and unwritten understandings from the FIELD OF FLOWERS Employees Handbook.

Excerpts are noted in regular type face. Unwritten understandings are in italics. Comments by the authors are noted in Sans Serif type.

Issue 1

Provide employees feedback on his or her work

All associates have the following rights: ...the right to have access to all useful, pertinent information about the enterprise and about one's particular job.... This includes the right to participate in the process or decision making related to one's work area.

If you have questions or concerns about anything related to your employment, talk with your Team Leader. That person will assist you in every way possible.

Issue 2

Provide a basis for salary increases and bonuses

All employees begin their careers with Field of Flowers at the same salary ($6.50 per hour). This applies to everyone: floral arrangers, delivery personnel, sales associates, and so on. The orientation period for every potential associate is based on the needs of that particular individual. Thus, the length of orientation varies from person to person. After orientation is complete, employees become level two associates and their salary is automatically raised to $8.50 per hour. After two years, level two associates become tenured associates and receive $8.50 per hour plus profit-sharing. Associates who have achieved tenured status will be beneficiaries of profit-sharing for any year in which profit-sharing is appropriate (according to the established corporate guidelines). Percentage of profit-sharing will be based upon earned income. Part-time and full-time associates will participate in profit-sharing. *All employees know daily sales figures and are provided complete financial disclosure once each year so that they understand the distribution of profit-sharing.*

Issue 3

Identify candidates for promotion

We believe in the benefits of advancing people from within the organization whenever possible. We recognize that this requires that numerous very able people be hired into entry level positions and be offered the opportunity to expand their knowledge.

The following sections of the Employee Handbook deal with termination. We have decided to place these sections under Issue 3 because they deal with termination (a form of demotion).

All tenured associates have the right to employment security. In keeping with its philosophy of long-term commitment to its associates, FIELD OF FLOWERS will consider layoffs of tenured associates only after all other remedies—including reduced profit expectations—have been exhausted. If work force reductions become necessary for the survival of the company, then a council of tenured associates will be formed to advise management as to the best manner in which to make those reductions. In the case of severe disciplinary action or dismissal for cause, tenured associates will have the right to demand peer review of such action. An elected Associates' Council will review such cases; they will have the authority to overturn or revise the action taken.

During the Orientation process, especially during the first 90 days of employment, Associates are expected to be attentive and interested in learning the procedures we follow. After the Trial Period ends and the Associate is raised to Associate II, they are expected to follow the guidelines and procedures that were a part of their Orientation/Training. Any Associate who deliberately and knowingly refuses to adhere to established procedures can be dismissed without following the usual measures that preclude termination without counseling and documentation.

Issue 4

Provide periodic direction to employee's work

FIELD OF FLOWERS' leadership provides feedback to employees by stating and constantly pursuing their mission, taking responsibility for processes, and working with employees to develop plans for the methods needed to achieve the FIELD OF FLOWERS mission.

A Service Example of Cross-Functional Management

FIELD OF FLOWERS has a statement of mission and values. This statement creates a culture in which leadership provides direction to employees. The statement appears below.

> In management, the first concern of the company is the happiness of the people who are connected with it. If the people do not feel happy and cannot be made happy, that company does not deserve to exist.
>
> — Ishikawa

The primary mission of FIELD OF FLOWERS is to provide stable, safe, fulfilling employment for our family of associates. We realize that the way to accomplish this is to be recognized by the community as the company, in our chosen field of endeavor, which provides the highest quality products and services to its customers.

We believe in the importance of constancy of purpose toward never-ending improvement of the processes which produce our products and services. We further believe that the leadership of the company must take responsibility for these processes. Associates must not be held accountable for improving results if they do not have the authority or the resources to change the processes which produce those results.

We must always be alert to the harm that can result from setting arbitrary numerical goals and standards without providing the methods for achieving them.

Issue 5

Provide an opportunity to give recognition, direction, and feedback to an employee regarding his or her work on special projects.

All associates are given opportunities to grow and develop in ways that are mutually beneficial to themselves and the company. Such growth and development can include special projects. It is the responsibility of management to set into motion and nurture the improvements and innovations developed by associates. This type of leadership will stimulate the intrinsic motivation of associates.

Issue 6

Identify an employee's needs for training, education, and skill or career development

The Management Team (top management of FIELD OF FLOWERS) accepts complete responsibility for accurately and adequately training all associates. By empowering associates with knowledge and skill, stress is reduced and their employment experience can be pleasant and rewarding.

We believe in vigorous programs for training and education so that our associates are able to grow as workers as well as in other aspects of their lives.

...training and a supportive attitude on the part of leadership, will empower front line associates to make decisions on their own.

Tuition reimbursement is available to associates with at least one year of service. Company approval is required prior to enrollment and will be determined on a case by case basis.

Issue 7

Provide an equitable, objective, defensible system that satisfies the requirement of the 1964 Civil Rights Act and the Equal Opportunity Commission guidelines of 1966 and 1970

We are committed to selecting the most qualified person for each position in our company. Our success is dependent upon our maintaining high standards and emphasizing "teamwork!" All personnel selections are in accordance with Equal Employment Opportunity guidelines.

Each employee contributes to FIELD OF FLOWERS' success; each will be treated fairly.

Issue 8

Provide a channel for communication that otherwise would probably not occur.

The company culture of FIELD OF FLOWERS promotes open, multi-way communication within and between all levels of employees. The perfor-

mance appraisal process at FIELD OF FLOW-ERS is a daily ongoing process of communication which constantly seeks to increase employees' ability to take pride in their work and joy in the outcome, and to optimize its interdependent system of stakeholders.

The study and development of the performance appraisal system was the first step (STANDARDIZE) of the SDSA cycle. The team progressed through the Do, Study, and Act stages and now continuously works on improvement of the performance appraisal system through application of the PDSA cycle.

Summary

Chapter 5 discusses Cross-Functional Management, Prong Three of the quality management model presented in this book. Cross-Functional Management is important because it weaves together the vertical (line) functions of management with the horizontal (interdepartmental) functions of management. Primary applications of Cross-Functional Management include quality management, cost management, delivery management, and personnel management. Other applications are new product development, sales management, and safety management.

Selecting cross-functional teams was discussed in this chapter. The members of the EC initially form cross-functional teams and select their leaders. The leader, who is an executive in charge of a function, recommends the members for the team, preferably no more than five people. It is not necessary for all team members to come from affected areas. All team members are trained in appropriate theory and practice.

In small organizations, one cross-functional team comprising all relevant executives can be established to coordinate and optimize all company-wide systems. In large organizations, one cross-functional team can be set up for each company-wide system, such as quality management, safety management, or personnel management. The EC reviews, manages, and coordinates all cross-functional teams. Cross-Functional Management reviews are conducted at least yearly by the cross-functional team leader.

Implementing Cross-Functional Management is difficult because of its interdisciplinary nature. To ensure the success of a cross-functional team, it is created with the expectation that it will be permanent and deal with continuous improvement of a company-wide system over the long term. Cross-functional team members learn to think in terms of the whole system, not just their areas. Communicating the results of the cross-functional team's work is extremely important.

Chapter 5 presents a use of Cross-Functional Management in a manufacturing company, Toyota Forklift. This manufacturer uses

CHAPTER 5   Cross-Functional Management (Prong Three)

Cross-Functional Management to deal with new product development.

An in-depth example of how a service company, Field of Flowers, used a cross-functional team to create its performance appraisal system is also discussed in this chapter.

Prong Four

B ackground

Policy Management is performed by turning the PDSA cycle to improve and innovate the methods responsible for the difference between corporate results and corporate targets or to change the direction of an organization. Corporate targets are set to allocate resources between corporate methods. Policy Management assumes that housekeeping, daily management, and Cross-Functional Management are at work in the organization.

Policy Management is accomplished through an interlocking system of committees (see Figure 6.2).

Purpose of this Chapter

The purpose of this chapter is to explain what is required to set policy, deploy policy, implement policy, study policy, provide feedback to employees on policy, and conduct Presidential Review of policy in an organization. Policy Management[1] (see the reference on the next page) is Prong Four of the quality management model presented in this book (see the Detailed Fork Model).

A Model for the Transformation of an Organization

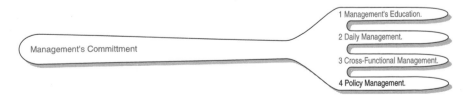

Management's Committment

1 Management's Education.

2 Daily Management.

3 Cross-Functional Management.

4 Policy Management.

Figure 6.1

Committee Structure for Policy Management

> **Executive Committee (EC)**
> Values and Beliefs
> Vision and Mission
> Draft Strategic Plan

> **Policy Deployment Committee (PDC)**
> Strategic Plan
> (top to bottom discussion)
> Draft Improvement Plans

> **Local Steering Committees (LST)**
> Improvement Plans
> (feedback and review)
> Projects

> **Project Teams**
> Projects
> (improvement and innovation of a process)

Figure 6.2

---

1. The material on policy management is drawn heavily from the following sources:

(1) Mizuno, Shigeru, *Management for Quality Improvement: The 7 New QC Tools*, Productivity Press (P.O. Box 3007, Cambridge, MA, 02140), 1988.

(2) Ishikawa, K., *What is Total Quality Control? The Japanese Way*, Prentice Hall (Englewood Cliffs, NJ) 1985, pp. 59 - 71.

(3) King, Bob, *Hoshin Planning: The Developmental Approach*, GOAL/QPC (Metheun, MA), 1989.

(4) Brunetti, Wayne, *Achieving Total Quality: Integrating Business Strategy and Customer Needs*, Quality Resources (One Water Street, White Plains, NY), 1993.

The authors would like to thank Francisco "Tony" Avello, Florida Power & Light Company, for his input into this section.

The authors take sole responsibility for the material presented in this section.

The Executive Committee (EC) is responsible for setting the strategic plan for the entire organization. That includes establishing values and beliefs, developing statements of vision and mission, and preparing a draft set of strategic objectives. The Policy Deployment Committee (PDC) is responsible for deploying the strategic objectives in the entire organization. That includes developing an improvement plan (set of short-term tactics) for each department. A Local Steering Team (LST) is responsible for implementing policy (short-term tactics) within a department by coordinating and managing project teams. Project teams implement policy through improvement and innovation of the processes highlighted for attention.

The Local Steering Teams conduct meetings with Project Teams, called Feedback and Review sessions, to learn about team activity, promote quality theory and tools, and manage and coordinate team activities to pursue company policy. The Policy Deployment Committee conducts meetings with Local Steering Committees, called Mini-SITCONS, to learn about team activity, promote quality theory and tools, coordinate and manage project teams to optimize company policy, and, if necessary, to reallocate resources between project teams (according to revised targets). Finally, the President meets with the leader of each department to understand the state of quality in the organization and to de-

171

termine if policy (strategic objectives) is being implemented throughout the organization.

Initial Presidential Review: Step 28

The President conducts an initial Presidential Review (see step 28 of the Detailed Fork Model) to determine the state of the organization and to develop a plan of action for the promotion of corporate policy. Presidential Reviews are high-level studies of an organization's departments by the President or Chief Executive Officer.[2]

During Presidential Reviews, the leaders of the departments explain to the President their mission and the status of projects emanating from the strategic and improvement plans. Normally, this information is conveyed through presentations. Much attention is devoted to the linkage between corporate and department strategies, and the progress toward the achievement of these strategies. Problems in planning and executing these strategies are discussed, and attempts are made to identify the causes of these problems. Through the Presidential Review, the President is able to evaluate the state of quality and management in the organization.

---

2. This section of the chapter was rewritten from material prepared by Mr. Francisco "Tony" Avello of Florida Power & Light Company, Miami, FL, 1992.

Reasons for
Conducting the
Presidential Review

Presidential Reviews are conducted for several reasons. First, they are conducted to determine the extent of achievement of organizational policy. Reviews are conducted to verify the implementation of improvement plans and to assess and improve the management process used to achieve the mission. In one company, the President found out that one of his policies had been completely misinterpreted, and the troops were marching in the opposite direction. The mistake was identified and quickly rectified to avert much wasted effort. This is not a rare occurrence in large organizations because information is filtered by each layer of management. Second, Presidential Reviews are conducted to determine the cost to the organization of achieving its strategic and improvement plans. Third, Presidential Reviews are conducted to prevent deterioration in methods not highlighted for attention in policy management, due to the reallocation of resources to methods highlighted for attention in policy management. Finally, Presidential Reviews identify the major problems facing the organization. The President tries to discover those problems that affect functional performance but cannot be solved at the functional level. Generally, these problems have to be addressed at the company level since the causes cross many organizational boundaries. In this way, no single function has the authority to promote solutions. Most major company problems are cross-functional and thus difficult to identify. Because of its cross-functional nature, the Presidential Review provides a significant opportunity to identify these problems. Once identified, these problems are turned over to appropriate cross-functional teams.

Benefits of Presidential Reviews

One benefit of Presidential Reviews is that they promote a dialogue between the President and mid-level management. This dialogue encourages an atmosphere of trust that helps bring out information about problems. The information provides an opportunity for the President to create joy in work and pride in the outcome for all employees.

Another benefit of Presidential Reviews is the insight they give to the President about the operations and culture of the organization. Frequently, this information is not available through normal channels of communication. Examples of information that can be gleaned by the President include the skill level of the managers and supervisors, the attitudes of employees toward improvement of methods, and employee morale. This information is necessary to promote the strategic and improvement plans.

The President will have a good understanding of the major problems facing the organization after a full round of Presidential Reviews. So, to a certain extent, he or she should have a good idea about the possible causes of problems. The President knows the areas that should be involved in the improvement activities. He or she should also know the attitudes and skills of employees in carrying out the strategic and improvement plans. Finally, he or she knows the level of training that will be needed throughout the organization to work on the strategic and improvement plans.

Barriers to the Presidential Review

Initially, the President may resist conducting Presidential Reviews due to demands on his or her time. All too often, there is a desire to obtain information from an executive summary. However, the executive summary does not provide sufficient information to establish or change the direction of the company. One company President tells the story of how he went from opposing Presidential Reviews to so thoroughly embracing them that he began to conduct half-day reviews on a quarterly basis with each of his departments.

Selecting the Departments and Topics to Review

Departments and topics are selected for Presidential Review by examining the policies and projects that were not successful in previous years. Underachieved policies and projects are considered failures of the management system. These problems identify the departments that are candidates for Presidential Review. It is important that the President doesn't assign fault for problems. Blame-fixing makes people defensive and unwilling to identify problems. It creates fear in the work place. The President takes responsibility for problems in the system.

Another way of selecting departments and/or topics for Presidential Review is to proceed as explained in the previous paragraph, but to review all departments. This has the advantage of not singling out any department's past failures, thus avoiding a threatening situation. One drawback to this approach is that more departments have to be reviewed than in the first alternative. Ultimately, the culture of the company and the existing organizational climate will dictate which alternative is best. In either scenario, the issue of not creating a threatening situation is an important one and is weighed carefully before deciding which approach to take.

Informing the Departments to be Reviewed

Once the topics and functions have been identified, the next step is to announce the reviews. This is done through a meeting of senior managers. The purpose of the reviews is explained in this meeting. The names of the departments that will participate in the reviews are announced, and the format of the reviews is discussed. Steps are taken to put the participating departments at ease. If needed, the President offers staff help in further clarifying the objectives, guidelines, and manner of the reviews. Also, this is a good time to define the ground rules to follow during the reviews.

Ground Rules for the Presidential Review

Probably the most important ground rule for Presidential Review is that the presenter submits his or her department's report at least one week prior to the review. This rule is usually resisted, since most presenters will make changes to their presentation until the last minute. However, as will become apparent in the next section, it is important to enforce this rule. Another important ground rule is using data to support the major, if not all, the points of the presentation. Since the reviewer will be using the presentation as a vehicle to acquire information for establishing company policies, the presentation should rely on facts as much as possible.

The presenting department is allowed to bring and use as many presenters as needed to fully explain the principal issues or to answer questions. The President usually invites managers from related departments to the review. This is done not only to make them aware of the important issues of that department, but also for them to get a glimpse of the review procedures and thus help them prepare for their own reviews. The atmosphere of the review is informal but serious.

Preparing for the Reviews

Proper preparation for a Presidential Review is important. Many reviews fail before they begin because of poor preparation by the President. Good reviews are borne out of careful study of the presenter's report before the reviews. This study allows the President to establish a focus for the review, identify issues needing clarification, and formulate questions.

It is critical to have a staff department help the President prepare for the reviews. Usually, this task is assigned to the Quality Department. However, it could be any department knowledgeable about the Presidential Review process and total quality management in general. The assigned department assists the President in fully understanding the present situation of the presenting department and in developing a list of topics or broad questions to ask the presenters. More specific questions will normally follow from the answers given by the presenters. The President conducts the review and becomes knowledgeable enough to conduct future reviews without extensive help. Therefore, a key task of the staff department assisting the President is to instruct and coach the President so that he or she can become a competent reviewer.

Conducting the Review

Usually, the review begins with a presentation by the management of a department. The presentation is followed by a question and answer period which is led by the President. It is customary to allow the presenter to finish the presentation without interruption, except for clarifying questions.

When the presenter has concluded, the President begins the question and answer period. It is his or her opportunity to probe deeply into issues to determine the possible causes of problems. Often, the President will be persistent and ask the same question several times to get the appropriate answer. For critical issues or when the answers are not provided, action items with due dates are established. The presenters demonstrate the results of the action items at a later date.

The following questions are examples of the type of questions the President might ask a presenter. They are offered here for illustration purposes only.

1. What is the mission of your department?

2. Does your department's mission support the company's mission?

3. How do you know if you are pursuing company policy?

4. What procedures do you follow when you discover that you are not pursuing company policy?

5. Can you show me an example of a corrective action you have taken when your department was not pursuing company policy?

6. How did you analyze the failure to pursue company policy?

7. How did you know if the corrective action was effective?

8. What are the major problems/opportunities of your department?

9. How do these problems/opportunities manifest themselves?

10. Can you give me an example?

11. What effects do these problems/opportunities have on your department and/or on your customers?

12. Who are your customers?

13. What needs and wants do they have?

14. How, and how often, do you assess their needs and wants?

15. Can you show me how you are en-suring the satisfaction of your cus-tomers' needs and wants?

The attitude of the President during the re-view is very important. Often, the President has to be persistent to obtain the answers he or she needs to make decisions. In some cas-es, the President pushes the presenters to obtain a desired performance level or be-havior. This may be seen as judgmental or harsh by the presenters. The President's job is to establish an atmosphere of teamwork, providing constructive criticism, examples of ideas for improvement, and/or where to go for help.

The staff department members and con-sultant helping the President during the review assume a low profile. They ask questions only at the request of the Presi-dent, after the President has finished his or her own questions.

After the reviews, the staff department and/or the consultant meets with the Pres-ident to identify his or her successful and unsuccessful actions and behaviors during the review. The purpose of this meeting is to instruct and coach the President to improve his or her skills as a reviewer. It is best to concentrate on only two to three items at one time and not tamper with the Presiden-tial Review process.

The most important determinant to a successful Presidential Review is whether the President can gain the trust of management. It is critical that the President guarantees that presenters will not be harmed if they disclose problems in their departments.

Another key to a successful review is the quality of the preparation by the President and his staff. If they learn all they can about the topic being reviewed, research and analyze the past accomplishments and failures of the department being reviewed, and focus on problem areas that offer good opportunities for improvement, they are more likely to create a positive review process.

Another important factor in a successful review is the assignment of action items to presenters when data is not provided as requested. Failure to assign action items when needed may communicate to the organization that mediocrity is acceptable.

It is more important to concentrate on process and results, not only results, in Presidential Reviews. The President helps the presenter see how poor results are most likely due to a deficiency in a management process. Also, the President sets an example by identifying and working to improve deficiencies in the Presidential Review process.

Policy Setting: Steps 29 and 30

Once the initial Presidential Review is complete, the President has information critical to setting policy. Policy Management entails the establishment of organizational values and beliefs, statements of vision and mission, strategic objectives (see step 29 of the Detailed Fork Model), and a set of integrated improvement plans (see step 30 of the Detailed Fork Model) for the departments.

Executive Committee (EC)

The members of the Executive Committee (EC) work to understand the pros and cons for transformation of the organization from the perspective of each stakeholder group. The top management of an organization asks the question "Does my organization have the motivation and energy necessary to make quality happen?" The data from this question is collected, summarized, and analyzed through a force field analysis. Recall, from Chapter 2, that force field analysis is a technique which lists the "forces for" and "forces against" a particular action or issue. After analysis, if the members of the EC determine that the "forces for" transformation outweigh the "forces against" transformation, they develop a strategic plan for transformation.

A strategic plan lists the long-term strategic objectives of an organization. Strategic objectives are based on a thorough analysis of statements of vision and mission, values and beliefs, organizational and environmental factors, crises, if any, key processes that affect stakeholders, and technology. Figure 6.3 depicts the relationship between the above six items and the strategic objectives.

Development of Strategic Objectives

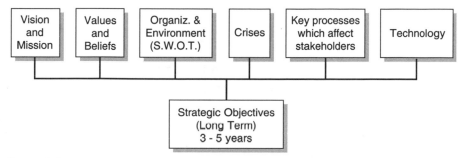

Figure 6.3

Statements of vision and mission. Dr. Deming's theory of management addresses the need to establish constancy of purpose toward improvement of product and service with a plan to become competitive, stay in business, and provide jobs (see point one of Dr. Deming's 14 points). Statements of vision and mission are starting points for constancy of purpose.

A vision statement is developed by the top management of an organization. It defines the organization's future state. It is a dream that comes from the "hearts" of top management. It should evoke emotion, be easily remembered, state a noble purpose, and create a rallying point for all concerned with the organization.

The mission statement reveals the current reason for the existence of an organization. It is developed by the top management of an organization. The mission statement provides a rallying point for all stakeholders.

Values and beliefs. A statement of the values and beliefs that govern an organization's culture is necessary to provide predictable uniformity and dependability to the decision-making process. This statement forms the foundation for the decision-making process. Values and beliefs are theories about life and organizations which have been modified and improved by cultural, educational, familial, organizational, and personal experiences. However, through the adoption of Dr. Deming's theory of management, an organization can develop a set of values and beliefs that form its foundation. The values and beliefs inherent in Dr. Deming's theory of management are as follows:

Manage to create a win-win environment, not a win-lose environment. The focus of a win-win environment is optimization of all stakeholders in the organization's system of interdependent stakeholders.

Manage to create intrinsic motivation, not extrinsic motivation. Intrinsic motivation is the individual's desire to do something for its own value, as opposed to extrinsic motivation, which relies on rewards for the individual.

Manage with a long-term process and results orientation, not with a short-term results-only orientation. Process and results
management promotes improvement and
innovation of organizational processes.
Highly capable processes facilitate prediction of the future and, consequently, a higher likelihood of achieving the organizational mission.

Manage to promote cooperation, not competition. In a competitive environment,
most people lose. The costs resulting from
competition are unknown and unknowable, but they are huge. Competition causes
individuals, or departments, to optimize
their own efforts at the expense of other
stakeholders. This form of optimization seriously erodes the performance of the system of interdependent stakeholders.

Organizational and environmental factors.
A SWOT analysis is used to assist the members of the EC in selecting the strategic objectives that ensure the best fit between the
internal strengths and weaknesses of an organization and the external opportunities
and threats that face an organization. A detailed description of how to perform a
SWOT analysis was presented in Chapter 2.
After the SWOT analysis is conducted, the
data collected is used in the development of
the strategic objectives of the organization.

Crises. The members of the EC determine if
any crises currently face the organization. If
one or more crises are currently threatening

the organization, management communicates this information to all stakeholders to create the energy necessary to improve and innovate quality. If no crises are known to be confronting the organization, management conducts a SWOT analysis to determine potential crises. Discovering crises in this fashion is an important job of top management. Again, it is necessary for leadership to isolate a crisis to generate the energy necessary to improve and innovate quality.

Key processes that affect stakeholders. Data is collected to determine the requirements important to the customers serviced by an organization (called "Voice of the Customer," see Appendix 1) and the requirements important to all levels of employees in the organization (called "Voice of the Business," see Appendix 2). Determination of these issues will help the members of the EC identify the key processes (methods), whose level of performance will affect the selection of strategic objectives.

"Voice of the Customer" and "Voice of the Business" data are summarized into a single prioritized list of the methods to be highlighted for attention through the strategic objectives. The tool used to prioritize customer and employee issues is called the Table of Tables (see Appendix 3).

Technology. The members of the EC collect data on technological advances of products and services in the industry, substitute products and services, future products and services, and management technology. All forms of technology are considered when establishing policy via strategic objectives.

Develop strategic objectives and a budget. The members of the EC utilize the information gathered in the above six areas to create a short list of three to five strategic objectives on which the organization will focus extra effort in the next three to five years, through policy management. Each of the six areas could potentially yield a crisis or a set of crises which are resolved through policy management.

The members of the EC establish an initial budget to allocate resources between strategic objectives. It is important that strategic plans identify all available resources (e.g., financial, human, and plant and equipment). Resources are allocated to methods by setting targets. Targets may be reset at a later date to optimize the interdependent system of stakeholders of an organization. Strategic objectives are things that will be done in addition to the regular functioning of the organization.

Policy Deployment Committee (PDC)

The members of the EC communicate to the members of the PDC the pros and cons for transformation, vision and mission statements, values and beliefs, and strategic objectives.

The members of the PDC develop a set of integrated improvement plans (step 30 in the Detailed Fork Model) to promote the strategic objectives. Improvement plans (tactics) prioritize processes (methods) for attention through policy management. Resources are allocated between methods by setting targets. An improvement plan usually follows a one-to-two-year time horizon. The members of the PDC utilize the following steps to construct a set of integrated improvement plans.

Step 1a. Develop the corporate improvement plans needed to promote the corporate strategic objectives. "Gap analysis" is used to study the root cause(s) of the difference between customer and employee requirements, and organizational performance for each strategic objective. The members of the PDC assign a group of staff personnel to study the gap for a particular strategic objective. The group might study the gap over time and determine that it is stable and contains only common variation. Next, they construct a Pareto diagram of the common causes of the gap, isolate the most significant common cause, and develop a cause-and-effect diagram. Then the staff personnel studies the relationship between the suspected root (common) cause and the size of the gap. If the staff personnel finds the relationship to be significant, they recommend a tactic for consideration as part of the organization's improvement plan to the members of the PDC.

The relationship between corporate strategic objectives and corporate improvement

plans (tactics) can be seen in Figure 6.4. Relationships are measured on the following
scale: 3 = direct relationship, 2 = indirect
relationship, 1 = some relationship, and
blank = no relationship.

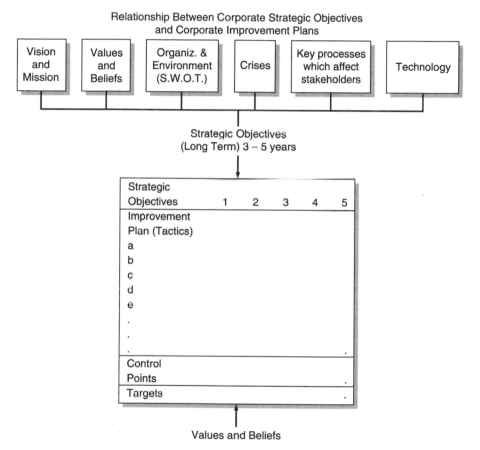

Figure 6.4

Every strategic objective is adequately serviced by one or more tactics. If a strategic
objective is not being serviced by any tactic
(or not adequately serviced), one or more

189

tactics are developed to service the strategic objective. All columns of the matrix in Figure 6.4 should contain at least one score of two or three.

Step 1b. Develop the departmental improvement plans (tactics) needed to promote the departmental strategic objectives.

Organizations need a mechanism for setting policy and allocating responsibility and resources in departments and divisions to promote corporate policy. Such a mechanism can be seen in Figure 6.5.

Setting Policy and Allocating Responsibility and Resources

Section A of Figure 6.5 provides departmental management an opportunity to create departmental vision and mission statements which promote the corporate vision and mission statements. Section B of Figure 6.5 lists the corporate strategic objectives (see the columns of Figure 6.4). Section C of Figure 6.5 lists the corporate improvement plans (tactics) (see the rows of Figure 6.4). Section D of Figure 6.5 list the departmental strategic objectives. Departmental management considers all the information utilized in developing the corporate strategic objectives when developing the departmental strategic objectives. Section E of Figure 6.5 shows the strength of relationships between corporate strategic objectives and departmental strategic objectives. Relationships are measured on the following scale: 3 = direct relationship, 2 = indirect relationship, 1 = some relationship, and blank = no relationship. Every

Setting Policy, and Allocating Responsibility and Resources

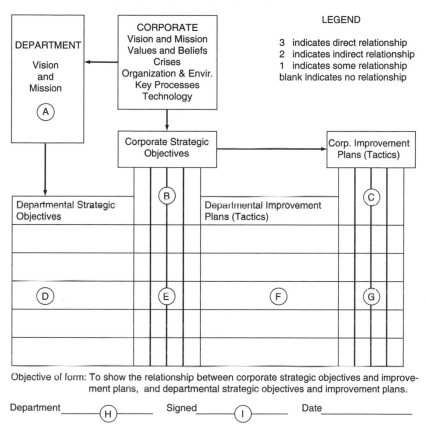

Figure 6.5
Source: Quality Improvement Department, FP&L, May 3, 1985

corporate strategic objective is adequately serviced by one or more departmental strategic objectives. If a corporate strategic objective is not being serviced, or adequately serviced, by any departmental strategic objectives, then one or more departments develop strategic objectives to service that corporate strategic objective. Section F of Figure 6.5 lists the departmental improvement plans (tactics) required to promote the corporate improvement plans (tactics). When entering this information, it is important to line up departmental improvement plans with the departmental strategic objectives they will promote. Finally, section G of Figure 6.5 shows the strength of relationships between corporate improvement plans and departmental improvement plans. Relationships are measured on the following scale: 3 = direct relationship, 2 = indirect relationship, 1 = some relationship, and blank = no relationship. Every corporate improvement plan is adequately serviced by one or more departmental improvement plans. If a corporate improvement plan is not being serviced or adequately serviced, by any departmental improvement plan, one or more departments develop improvement plans to service that corporate improvement plan. Section H of Figure 6.5 indicates the name of the department or division filling out the form. Section I of Figure 6.5 shows the signature of the departmental manager responsible for setting policy.

Step 2. The members of the PDC select and operationally define control items and targets for the corporate improvement plans (see Figure 6.4). These control points and targets are deployed into departmental control points and targets. Targets are used to allocate resources for improvement projects to departments.

The members of the PDC ask the following questions:[3]

1. Have the control points used to monitor improvement plans been operationally defined?

2. Have targets been assigned to projects to optimize the corporate strategic objectives?

Step 3. The members of the PDC review and prioritize the projects called for in the improvement plans. The members of the PDC reach consensus on the priorities assigned to methods. They ask the following questions:[4]

1. Are priority projects well defined?

2. Will taking care of these priority projects help achieve the strategic objectives?

3. Are there better ways to achieve the strategic objectives?

4. Have the costs associated with pursuing the strategic objectives been studied?

5. Have the most appropriate projects been highlighted for study in the improvement plans?

6. Are projects defined with enough specificity so that everyone understands them?

---

3. These questions have been adapted from Mizuno, p. 106.
4. The questions in this section are paraphrased from Mizuno, p. 106.

7. Were projects discussed with relevant people and groups?

8. Were constraints on methods considered by the PDC?

9. Has the effectiveness of the projects been studied?

10. Are sufficient resources available for the projects?

Step 4. The members of the PDC communicate the projects that emanate from corporate and departmental improvement plans to the Local Steering Teams (LSTs), including the allocation of resources. The members of the PDC and an LST come to consensus on projects, targets, and resources in meetings called catchball sessions.

Local Steering Teams (LSTs)

The members of the LSTs are responsible for coordinating and carrying out the projects set out in the corporate and departmental improvement plans. The members of the PDC and LSTs should reach consensus on the priorities assigned to methods via targets that allocate resources. The members of LSTs ask the following questions:[5]

1. Are priority projects well defined?

2. Will taking care of these priority projects help achieve the improvement plans and strategic objectives?

---

5. The questions in this section are paraphrased from Mizuno, p. 106.

3.   Are there better ways to achieve the
     strategic objectives?

Policy Deployment: Step 31

The strategic objectives and improvement
plans are deployed by the members of the
PDC through assignment of responsibility
for action to people or groups of people in
departments (see step 31 of the Detailed
Fork Model). The assignment of responsibility is discussed by the members of the PDC
and LST in meetings called Mini-SITCONS.
Mini-SITCONS consider the costs to improve and innovate methods. After costs
have been identified, it may be necessary to
renegotiate project budgets. This process
continues until all parties reach a consensual
agreement on projects; again, this is called
catchball. Finally, the members of the PDC
ensure that the agreed-upon projects incorporate the information determined in the Table of Tables.

The assignment of responsibility for a
project to a manager creates an opportunity
to conduct a project that will result in improved or innovated "best practice" methods, the allocation of necessary resources,
and an obligation to predict the contribution of projects to strategic objectives.

A tool that can be used to track the contribution of departmental improvement plans in the pursuit of a corporate objective is the flag diagram. A flag diagram[6] is used to monitor the contribution of departmental targets toward a global corporate target (see Figure 6.6).

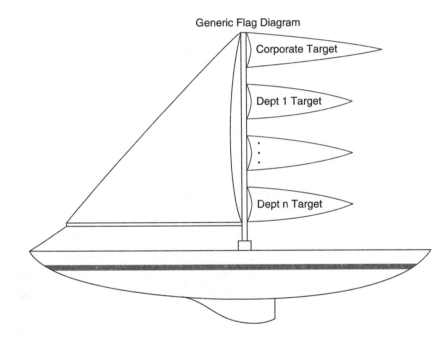

Generic Flag Diagram

Corporate Target

Dept 1 Target

Dept n Target

Figure 6.6

---

6. The material on the flag system was developed from the following sources:
    (1) Kano, Dr. Noriaki, *Second Report on TQC at Florida Power & Light Company*, (Miami, FL), October 1, 1986, pp. 3 and 34.
    (2) Aldecocea, Leo, *A Flag System Application for Monitoring Timeliness of Installation for a Daily Process*, University of Miami (Coral Gables, FL), May 4, 1990.

1. Additive flag system. In some applications of the flag system, corporate targets are the summation of departmental targets. When targets are additive, it is easy to determine how to allocate resources between projects by targets. If all departments meet or exceed the targets pertaining to a particular corporate objective, the corporate objective(s) will be achieved.

2. Nonadditive flag system. In other applications of the flag system, corporate targets are not the summation of departmental targets. When targets are not additive, it is difficult to determine how to allocate resources between projects by targets. If all divisions meet or exceed the targets pertaining to a particular corporate objective, it is unknown if the corporate objective will be achieved. In this case, knowledge and experience are required to determine the relationships between corporate objectives and their targets.

For example, progress toward a corporate objective of "continue to improve reliability of service to customers" could be tracked through the control point "number of minutes of downtime per year" into departments providing service to customers (see Figure 6.7). An integrated set of project targets would be set (see Figure 6.7) to allocate resources to the departments for projects to optimize the organization in respect to "continue to improve reliability of service to customers."

197

Example of a Flag Diagram

Corporate Improvement Plan (Tactic):
"Continue to improve reliability of service to customers"

Corporate Control Point:
"Number of minutes of down time per year"

Legend: ● = actual
100 = target

Department 1........(50% of reduction)........

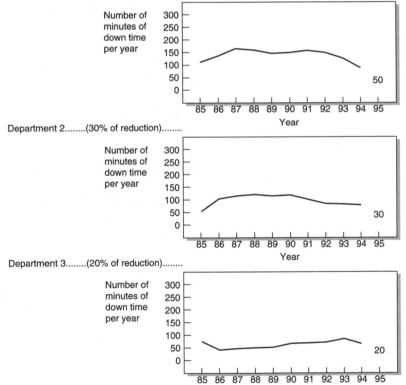

Department 2........(30% of reduction)........

Department 3........(20% of reduction)........

Figure 6.7

Deployment of an improvement plan project is completed when a project team has been assigned responsibility to improve or innovate a method. Figure 6.8 shows the projects, channels of communication, type of coordination, and resources necessary to implement policy in a department. Column A of Figure 6.8 shows departmental strategic objectives (see section D of Figure 6.5). Column B of Figure 6.8 shows the departmental improvement plans (tactics) needed to promote the departmental strategic objectives (see section F of Figure 6.5). Column C of Figure 6.8 shows the projects necessary for each departmental strategic objective. Each manager assigned a project must sign the appropriate line of column C indicating his or her acceptance of the project. Column D shows the channels of communication and types of coordination between departments needed to carry out the projects shown in column C. The manager of each department named as a necessary supporter of a project must sign the appropriate line of column D, indicating his or her willingness to assist in the conduct of the project. Column E shows the *additional* financial and human resources needed to carry out the projects shown in column C.

The members of an LST ask the following questions of all project team members:[7]

---

7. The questions in this section are paraphrased from Mizuno, p. 106.

Implementation of Policy in a Department

Departmental Strategic Objectives	Departmental Improvement Plan (Tactics)	Project	Other Depts. Affected/ Coordination Needed	Resources • Dollars • People
Ⓐ	Ⓑ	Ⓒ	Ⓓ	Ⓔ

Figure 6.8
Source: Florida Power & Light Company.

1. Are information channels between all relevant people and groups open to promote the improvement plan?

2. Has a detailed schedule been set up for carrying out the improvement plan?

Policy Implementation: Step 32

Policy is implemented in two ways. First, policy is implemented when teams work on projects to improve and/or innovate

processes. Second, policy is implemented when departments use the revised
processes and measure their results in respect to improvement plans and strategic
objectives.

The members of the EC assign responsibility for the promotion of each strategic objective to a high-level executive. The executive
removes any impediments to progress for
his or her strategic objective. Furthermore,
the executive coordinates efforts in respect
to the strategic objective throughout the organization. Finally, the members of the
PDC, in conjunction with the members of
various LSTs, may have to modify improvement plans as they proceed over time.

Policy Feedback and Review: Step 33

Periodic management reviews are conducted at two levels. First, the members of the
EC review progress toward each strategic
objective (and its improvement plans)
monthly. Brief presentations for each strategic objective are made by the high-level executive responsible for that strategic objective. Twice a year, each strategic objective is
selected for a detailed management review.
The detailed review probes very deeply
into the issues surrounding a strategic objective. The members of the EC insist that all
process modifications are supported by
sound analysis. This may require that action items be assigned to the high-level ex-

ecutive responsible for a strategic objective. The members of the EC also follow up on the action items. Second, the members of the PDC and of appropriate LSTs review progress for each project. The purpose of these reviews is to provide feedback to project team members that promotes process improvement efforts. The members of the PDC make sure that all process modifications are supported by sound analysis. This may require that action items be assigned to the members of a project team. The members of the PDC also follow up on the action items.

The members of the EC, PDC, or appropriate LSTs ask the following questions of project team members:

1. Does your organization have a vision statement and a mission statement?

2. Do you know what they are?

3. Do you understand how you can contribute to the vision and mission of your organization?

4. Does your department have vision and mission statements?

5. Do you know what they are?

6. Do you understand how you can contribute to the vision and mission of your department?

7. Do you understand how you can contribute to the vision and mission of the department? Organization? How do you know?

8. Do you understand the methods by which you will achieve the vision and mission of your department? organization?

9. Do you know which methods are most critical to pursue the vision and mission of your department? Organization?

10. Do you know the aims of these methods?

11. Do the aims of these methods support the aims of your department? organization?

12. Are these methods necessary?

13. What are the critical control items and control points for these methods?

14. Have the critical control items and control points been operationally defined?

15. Have you used the SDSA cycle to standardize methods?

16. Have you used the PDSA cycle to improve and innovate methods?

17. Do you understand who the customers of these methods are?

18. Do you understand the needs of those customers?

19. Do you know who the suppliers of these methods are?

20. Do you understand the needs of those suppliers?

21. Do you understand how these methods interact with other methods in

your department? Organization? How do you know?

22. Have you been trained in team skills and basic quality improvement tools?

23. Have you received training in the methods critical to your job?

24. Is your training in job skills updated as your job changes over time?

25. Have training manuals been updated as jobs change over time?

26. Do you receive feedback on the performance of the methods with which you work on a continuous basis?

27. Do you feel ownership of the methods with which you work?

28. Do you take pride in your work?

29. Do you take joy in the outcome of your work? How do you know?

30. Are you an empowered employee? How do you know?

31. Does your supervisor lead you in the conduct of planned experiments aimed at improvement and innovation of methods?

32. Do you have latitude to modify the methods you use on your job to take advantage of your unique skills and abilities?

33. Do you need the latitude you have in respect to a method?

34. Can all of your colleagues who perform a particular method produce equal outcomes?

35. Do you trust your supervisor to support the decisions you make within the latitude given to you in respect to a particular method?

36. Is your supervisor working toward eliminating fear in your department? Organization? How do you know?.

37. Are you implementing the improvement plan and/or projects per schedule?

38. Are records being kept of quality improvement efforts?

39. Are you revising the improvement plan as necessary?

The members of the EC and PDC ask the following questions of themselves:

1. Are we effectively conducting management reviews?

2. Are we improving and innovating the management review process?

3. Are methods being standardized and revised as required by the improvement plan?

Presidential Review: Step 34

Finally, the President conducts the Presidential Review (see step 34 of the Detailed Fork Model) of the major areas within the organization. Department managers present their efforts using the Quality Improvement story format. The purpose of the Presidential Review is to collect information used to establish the quality strategy and goals of the organization and to deter-

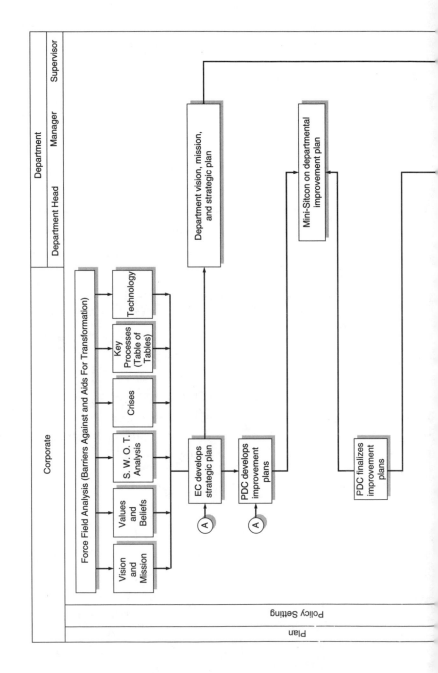

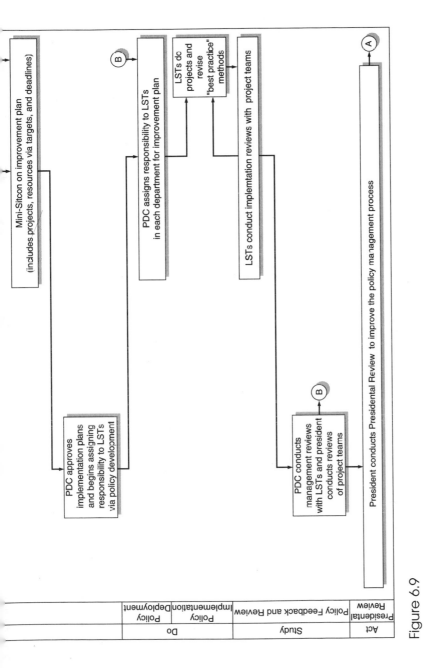

Mini-Sitcon on improvement plan (includes projects, resources via targets, and deadlines)

PDC approves implementation plans and begins assigning responsibility to LSTs via policy development

PDC assigns responsibility to LSTs in each department for improvement plan

LSTs do projects and revise "best practice" methods

LSTs conduct implemtation reviews with project teams

PDC conducts management reviews with LSTs and president conducts reviews of project teams

President conducts Presidental Review to improve the policy management process

	Do		Study	Act
	Policy Deployment	Policy Implementation	Policy Feedback and Review	Presidental Review

Figure 6.9

mine progress toward presidential policy. Presidential Reviews provide input for setting policy for the following year (see step 29 of the Detailed Fork Model). See the section of this chapter on "Initial Presidential Review" for details.The management system is improved with each successive policy management cycle.

Flowchart of Policy Management

An integrated flowchart depicting the relationship between the PDSA cycle and the five steps of policy management, and corporate and department responsibility for policy management, is shown in Figure 6.9

Relationship Between Policy Management and Daily Management

The relationship between policy management and daily management can be understood by viewing an organization as a tree. The vision is the root system, the mission is the trunk, the strategic objectives yield the major branches, and the improvement plans are smaller branches emanating out of the strategic objective branches. As expertise is developed with policy management methods, they are moved into daily management methods.

Frequently, employees claim that they do not have time for policy management due to the demands of their daily routine. Doing Daily Management and Cross-Functional Management removes non-value-added daily routine to free up time for policy management.

Personal Example of Policy Management

This section of the chapter presents the application of policy management to a person's life (organization). All the steps of policy management are used in this practical example, which demonstrates how to implement this detailed procedure. Bart is a 40-year-old manager in a large company. For the most part, his life has gone according to his plans. He is a respected manager, earns a comfortable salary, and is reasonably happy in his personal and family life. As he enters his forties, Bart begins to wonder whether he can improve his situation. Stimulated by what he is involved in at work, he decides to apply the principles of quality management to his life.

Bart's application of policy management follows.

(1) Policy Setting. Policy setting is illustrated below.

**Pros and Cons
to Transformation**

Bart performs a force field analysis and asks himself the following question: "Do I have the energy necessary to do quality management in my life?" From the force field analysis, he finds the aids for change to be more compelling than the barriers against change (see Figure 6.10). Bart decides to apply policy management in his life.

209

Force Field Analysis

Aids for Change	Barriers Against Change
Some dissatisfaction with my current life situation	No time to establish a policy management plan
Complaints from spouse, daughter, and brother	Family, friends, and colleagues will think I am a lunatic
Need to be more efficient and productive at work	

Figure 6.10

Values and Beliefs

Bart feels that the values and beliefs embodied in Dr. Deming's theory of management are completely consistent with his own, so he adopts these values and beliefs.

Vision and Mission

Bart's personal vision and mission define his future desired state and his current reason for existence.

Personal Vision: To be at peace with my world and to generate positive energy into the universe.

Personal Mission: To continuously improve my mind, body, and relationships.

Organizational and Environmental Factors

Bart conducts a SWOT analysis of himself. An abbreviated listing of strengths, weaknesses, opportunities, and threats is shown below.

Strengths: honest, forthright, mature, intelligent, excellent educational background, inquisitive, considerate, willing to help others with their problems, physically healthy, excellent communicator, strong support system of family and friends, well-established and ingrained values and beliefs, financially secure, professionally secure, able to stay focused, capable of retaining many facts until a strategy emerges, open to new ideas, resources available for self-improvement,...

Weaknesses: moderate swings in mood (too much common variation in a stable system), high cholesterol, twenty-five pounds overweight, unilingual, resents working in non-productive groups, not good at understanding other people's viewpoints, inability to change own behavior, poor short-term memory, low frustration tolerance,...

Opportunities: excellent business contacts, professional opportunities expanding, excellent system of personal mentors, increased ability to travel,...

Threats: increased demands to spend time working at the expense of personal life, parents passing away and not being prepared for the loss, the unknown and unknowable risks of life,...

Crises

The potential crisis known to Bart is diminution in health due to high weight and cholesterol.

Key Processes

"Voice of the Customer" and "Voice of the Business" analyses help prioritize processes (methods) for improvement attention. The purpose of these analyses is to provide cus-

211

tomer and personal (employee) input into the determination of strategic objectives.

Voice of the Customer

Bart surveys each of his stakeholders and asks them to answer the following question: "From your perspective, what requirements must I surpass to pursue my mission statement?" Data is collected from each individual. All issues that emerge from this analysis are quantified on a "dynamite" scale; the scale ranges from 1 stick of dynamite (unimportant or done well) to 5 sticks of dynamite (very important and not done well). The dynamite scale was developed to create data that can be averaged.[8] The "dynamite" data is being used to impart a "feel" for which issues are priority issues in Bart's pursuit of his mission. The "dynamite" data was analyzed using Pareto diagrams.

Spouse

The spouse's survey indicates 17 separate items of concern which are grouped into four subcategories: "Child care responsibility," "Home care responsibility," "Finances," and "Time allocation." All 17 items are rated on the dynamite scale (see Figure 6.11).

A Pareto analysis of the priority rankings shown in Figure 6.11 indicates that 36.6% of the spouse's issues involve household chores: "shop at supermarket," "shop at drug store," and "go to the dry cleaners" (see Figure 6.12). Therefore, "Home care re-

---

8. The authors realize that they are taking liberties with the scale of the data.

Personal Example of Policy Management

Voice of the Customer for Spouse

Category	Customer Ranking Survey Results (dynamite scale)
(a) Child care responsibility	
1. Drive child to/from school	1
2. Prepare child's dinner	2
3. Care for ill child	2
4. Help child with homework	1
(b) Home care responsibility	
1. Shop at supermarket	5
2. Shop at drug store	5
3. Go to dry cleaner	5
4. Sort clothes for wash	1
5. Make bank deposits	4
(c) Finances	
1. Prepare household accounts	1
2. Generate family income	1
3. Manage expense control	1
(d) Time allocation	
1. Decrease work time	4
2. Increase family time	2
3. Increase play time with child	2
4. Decrease business travel	2
5. Increase pleasure travel	2

Figure 6.11

sponsibility" is the spouse's critical area of concern.

Child

The child's survey indicates three items of concern (see Figure 6.13).

A Pareto analysis of the child's issues indicates that "increase play time" is the most critical area of concern; it accounted for 44% of the child's issues (see Figure 6.14).

Parents and Brother

The parents' and brother's survey indicates several items of concern (see Figure 6.15).

213

Pareto Analysis of Spouse's Voice of the Customer Data

Category	Rank	%	Cum. %	
Shop at supermarket	5	12.2	12.2*	36.6% of
Shop at drug store	5	12.2	24.4*	spouse's issues
Go to dry cleaner	5	12.2	36.6*	involve household
Decrease work time	4	9.6	46.2	chores
Make bank deposits	4	9.6	55.8	
Increase family time	2	4.9	60.7	
Increase play time with child	2	4.9	65.6	
Decrease business travel	2	4.9	70.5	
Increase pleasure travel	2	4.9	75.4	
Prepare child's dinner	2	4.9	80.3	
Care for ill child	2	4.9	85.2	
Drive child to/from school	1	2.45	87.65	
Help child with homework	1	2.45	90.10	
Sort clothes for wash	1	2.45	92.55	
Prepare household accounts	1	2.45	95.00	
Generate family income	1	2.45	97.45	
Manage expense control	1	2.45	99.90	
TOTAL...41		99.90		

Figure 6.12

Voice of the Customer for Child

Category	Customer Ranking Survey Results (dynamite scale)
Child	
(a) Increase play time	4
(b) Relax sleep over rules	2
(c) Decrease food restrictions	3

Figure 6.13

A Pareto analysis of the parents' and brother's concerns shows that 45% of all issues directly involve the brother (see Figure 6.16). The brother's three issues are: "share private feelings and dreams," "increase private time together," and "support each other."

Personal Example of Policy Management

Pareto Analysis of Child's Voice of the Customer Data

Category	Rank	%	Cum. %	
Increase play time	4	44	44*	44% of
Decrease food restrictions	3	33	77	child's issues
Relax sleep over rules	2	23	100	involve play
TOTAL...................................9		100		

Figure 6.14

Voice of the Customer for Parents and Brother

Category	Customer Ranking Survey Results (dynamite scale)
(a) Father	
1. Increase private time together	3
2. Go to sporting events together	2
3. Work on car together	2
4. Work on garden together	2
(b) Mother	
1. Determine common Interests	4
2. Increase private time together	3
(c) Brother	
1. Increase private time together	4
2. Share private feelings and dreams	5
3. Learn to support each	4

Figure 6.15

Voice of the Business

The Voice of the Business seeks to answer the following question:

"What requirements (e.g., concerns and fears) do I have in respect to pursuit of my mission?" Bart compiles a list of 11 issues that are critical to the fulfillment of his mission (see Figure 6.17).

215

Pareto Analysis of Parents and Brother Voice of the Customer Data

Category	Rank	%	Cum.	%
Brother – Share private feelings and dreams	5	17	17*	45% of
Brother – Increase private time together	4	14	31*	issues
Brother – Learn to support each	4	14	45*	involve
Mother – Determine common interests	4	14	59	brother
Mother – Increase private time together	3	10	69	
Father – Increase private time together	3	10	79	
Father – Go to sporting events together	2	7	86	
Father – Work on car together	2	7	93	
Father – Work on garden together	2	7	100	
TOTAL..29		100		

Figure 6.16

Voice of the Business

1) Increase pleasure travel with spouse
2) Increase private study time
3) Maintain study group time
4) Increase play time with child
5) Increase fun time with friends
6) Increase exercise time
7) Decrease body weight
8) Plan and shoot fireworks displays
9) Plan and execute special events
10) Increase private time with spouse
11) Improve financial security

Figure 6.17

These 11 issues are rated in respect to severity, urgency, trend, and importance to customer (see the prioritization matrix in Figure 6.18). The ratings are then multiplied to obtain a total score for each issue.

The items in the matrix are arranged in descending order of priority (see Figure 6.19).

Personal Example of Policy Management

Prioritization Matrix of the Voice of the Business

LEGEND:
(The Voice of the Business considers the existing system of
relationships between Bart and his environment.)

Severity   (1 = low severity;   5 = high severity)
Urgency   (1 = low urgency;   5 = high urgency)
Trend   (1 = steep positive trend;   2 = slight positive trend; 3 = flat;
    4 = slight negative trend;   5 = steep negative trends)
Importance to Customer (1 = unimportant to customer;
    5 = important to customer)

Category	Severity	Urgency	Trend	Import to Customer	TOTAL SCORE
(1) Inc. travel with spouse	1	1	2	3	6
(2) Inc. private study time	1	1	4	5	20
(3) Mntn study group time	1	1	2	5	10
(4) Inc. play with child	3	3	4	4	144
(5) Inc. fun with friends	1	1	2	3	6
(6) Inc. exercise time	3	3	3	5	130
(7) Dec. body weight	4	4	4	4	256
(8) Fireworks displays	1	1	2	1	2
(9) Special events	1	1	3	3	9
(10) Inc. time with spouse	2	2	4	5	80
(11) Imp. financial security	1	1	3	3	9

Figure 6.18

A Pareto analysis was done to the data in Figure 6.19 (see Figure 6.20).

Four of the 11 issues account for 90.7% of Bart's issues. These include "decrease body weight," "increase play time with child," "increase exercise time," and "increase time with spouse."

Table of Tables

The prioritized lists of issues from the "Voice of the Customer" and "Voice of the Business" studies are combined into one prioritized list in the rows of Figure 6.21.

217

Ranking of Voice of the Business Data

Category	Severity	Urgency	Trend	Importance to Customer	TOTAL SCORE
(7) Dec. body weight	4	4	4	4	256
(4) Inc. play with child	3	3	4	4	144
(6) Inc. exercise time	3	3	3	5	130
(10) Inc. time with spouse	2	2	4	5	80
(2) Inc. private study time	1	1	4	5	20
(3) Mntn. study group time	1	1	2	5	10
(9) Special events	1	1	3	3	9
(11) Imp. financial security	1	1	3	3	9
(1) Inc. travel with spouse	1	1	2	3	6
(5) Inc. fun with friends	1	1	2	3	6
(8) Fireworks displays	1	1	2	1	2

Figure 6.19

Pareto Analysis of the Voice of the Business Data

Category	Total Score	%	Cum. %
(7) Dec. body weight	256	38.1	38.1
(4) Inc. play with child	144	21.4	59.5
(6) Inc. exercise time	130	19.3	78.8
(10) Inc. time with spouse	80	11.9	90.7
(2) Inc. private study time	20	3.0	93.7
(3) Mntn. study group time	10	1.5	95.2
(9) Special events	9	1.3	96.5
(11) Imp. financial security	9	1.3	97.8
(1) Inc. travel with spouse	6	0.9	98.7
(5) Inc. fun with friends	6	0.9	99.6
(8) Fireworks displays	2	0.3	99.9
TOTAL	672	99.9	

Figure 6.20

The *importance to customer* scale shows that "decrease body weight," "increase exercise time," "household chores," and "increase playtime with child" are important to customers and Bart (see Figure 6.21). The *current level of performance* scale shows a large discrepancy (gap) between desired requirements and actual performance for "decrease body weight" (see Figure 6.22), "increase exercise time" (see Figure 6.23), and "household chores" (see Figure 6.24); see Figure 6.21.

The *desired level of importance* scale shows an urgency to improve "decrease body weight," "increase exercise time," and "household chores" (see Figure 6.21). Finally, the *total weight* scale shows the need to focus attention on "decrease body weight" (total weight = 25), "increase exercise time" (total weight = 20), and "household chores" (total weight = 25) in Bart's strategic objectives (see Figure 6.21).

The processes that form Bart's life are listed in the columns of Figure 6.21.

The cells of Figure 6.21 show the strength of the relationships between the "Voice of the customer" and "Voice of the Business" issues and the processes that form Bart's life.

The Table of Tables reveals that "weight" (priority = 135), "exercise" (priority = 135), and "shared responsibilities" (priority = 80.34) are the processes that must receive attention in Bart's strategic objectives if he is to surpass the needs and wants of his customers and himself (see the bottom row of Figure 6.21).

Partial Listing of Methods Which Are Important to Bart

LEGEND:

Symbol	Meaning	Score
●	Very important and not done well	3
○	Moderately important and not done well	2
△	Slightly important and not done well	1
	Unimportant or done well	0

Needs & Wants	Weight (Fitness)	Diet (Food Intake)	Exercise	Joy in work (Occupation)	Revenue	Travel (Leisure)	Entertainment	Education (Learning)	Training	Spiritual	Self Esteem (Psychological)	Well being	Joy	Love (Relationships)	Communication	Fun	Sharing responsibility	Importance to customer or employee (A)	Current level or importance to customer or employee (B)	Desired level of performance by management (C)	Total Weight = A(C/B)
Voice of the Customer																					
To become healthy with a low degree of variation																					
a. Decrease body weight	●	△	●					△			△	△						5	1	5	25
b. Increase exercise time	●		●									△						4	1	5	20
To continually improve and innovate my personal relationships																					
Voice of the Business																					
a. Spouse - Household chores													△				●	5	1	5	25
b. Daughter - Play time (increase play time with child)							△				△		○	●	●	●	○	4	3	2	2.67
c. Brother - Increase communication													○	○	●			1	3	2	0.67
d. Spouse - Increase time with spouse						●	●						●	●	●	●		1	4	2	0.50
To increase my knowledge																					
To increase and stabilize my financial resources																					
To be a good citizen																					
	135	25	135	0	0	1.5	4.17	25	0	0	27.67	45	33.18	10.85	11.52	9.51	80.34				

Figure 6.21

220

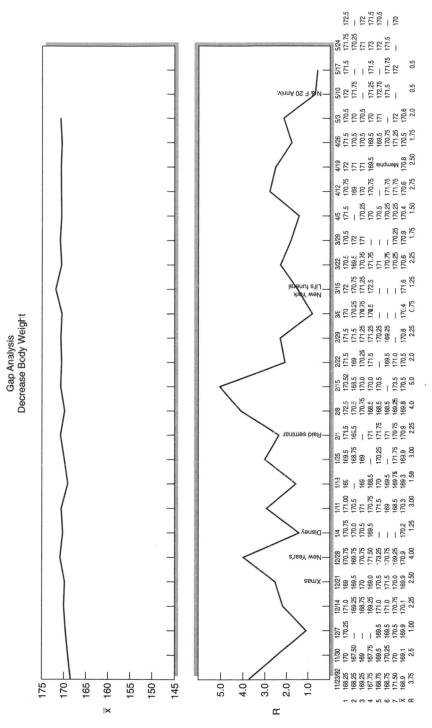

Figure 6.22

221

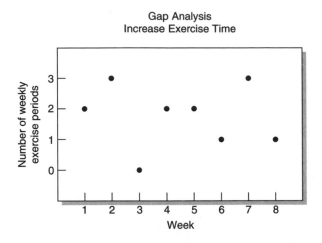

Figure 6.23

Technology

Bart realizes that using a treadmill at home—as opposed to jogging outside—makes him want to exercise more.

Develop Strategic Objectives

Bart's strategic objectives are:

1. To become healthy
2. To continually improve personal relationships

They emerge from an analysis of Bart's vision and mission statements, his values and beliefs, a SWOT analysis of his life, the crises Bart faces, the key processes that have to be improved to delight Bart's stakeholders, and technological issues that might affect Bart's life. All of the above sources can generate a crisis (or crises) which is addressed in the strategic objectives.

Develop the Improvement Plans

Bart brainstorms a list of the barriers that prevent him from becoming healthier as part of a "gap" analysis. The list includes

Personal Example of Policy Management

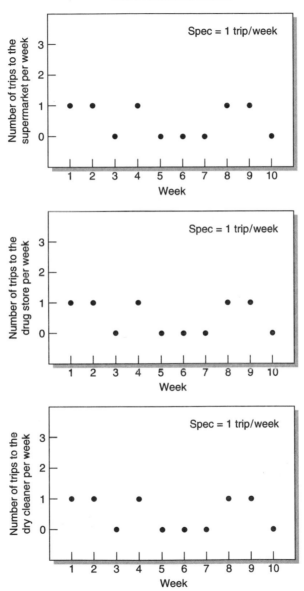

Figure 6.24

the following potential causes: too much body weight, too little exercise, unbalanced diet, too much stress, and too little sleep. An analysis of the interrelationships between the potential causes indicates that too little exercise and an unbalanced diet are the root causes which affect poor health in Bart's life (see Figure 6.25).

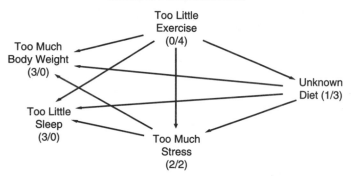

Interrelationship Diagram
Causes of Diminished Health

Figure 6.25
The arrows on the graph indicate the direction of cause to effect relationships; for example, "too much body weight." "Too much body weight" and "too little sleep" are processes which cannot be easily improved because they are effected by other causes of diminished health. However, "too little exercise" and "unbalanced diet" are processes which are root causes of diminished health.

Bart collects data on the barriers that prevent him from improving his personal relationships for a two-month period as part of a "gap" analysis. The barriers include the following potential causes: failure to share responsibilities (house care, child care, time allocation), moderate swings in mood, not good at understanding other people's viewpoints, poor short-term memory, low frustration tolerance, and increased demand to spend time at work. Figure 6.26 shows the frequency of occurrence of each barrier and that failure to share house care responsibilities is the most significant cause which affects Bart's personal relationships.

Pareto Analysis of Personal Relationships

Cause of poor relationships	#	%	Cum. %
responsibilities	52	72	72
mood	4	6	78
viewpoints	1	1	79
memory	2	3	82
frustration	12	17	99
time	1	1	100
Total	72	100	

Figure 6.26

The above "gap analyses" indicate that Bart needs to construct improvement plans to deal specifically with developing an exercise regimen, eating a nutritious diet, and sharing house care responsibilities, if he wants to surpass his strategic objectives.

Bart operationally defines control points and establishes targets for an exercise regimen, a dietary plan, and house care responsibilities; in particular, going to the supermarket, drug store, and dry cleaner. The purpose of the targets is to allocate the resources available to Bart between his improvement plan tactics. In this case, the targets are based on medical science and years

CHAPTER **6** **Policy Management (Prong Four)**

Control Points and Targets

Strategic Objective	Improvement Plan (Tactics)	Control Point	Target
To become healthy	develop an exercise regimen	# of exercise periods/week	3
	live a healthy diet	morning weight/day	145
To continually	do supermarket shopping	# trips/week	1
improve personal	do drug store shopping	# trips/week	1
relationships	go to dry cleaner	# trips/week	1

Figure 6.27

of experience with the chores. Control points and targets are shown in Figure 6.27.

(2) Policy Deployment. Responsibility for the three projects discussed in policy setting are assigned to Bart. The following section presents the methods that will be deployed in his improvement plan..

1. An Exercise Regimen:

Bart's method for improving his exercise regimen was discussed in Daily Management, Chapter 4.

2. A Dietary Plan:

PLAN (developing a plan)—A dietary plan (method) is developed to suit Bart's requirements and tastes. The plan calls for the advanced preparation of a weekly menu which Bart will carry at all times. The menu considers Bart's business travel schedule.

A target weight of 145 pounds was determined by Bart's physician as being his most healthy weight. It is predicted that the plan will achieve the targeted value of 145 pounds with minimal variation within an 8.4-month time frame (see Figure 6.28).

Dietary Plan

Target weight:
Current weight = 170 pounds
Target weight = 145 pounds
(Lose 25 pounds) –> Based on doctor's
                                    advice

Target Time frame: 10 Months
Rational for target time frame: Must lose 90,000 calories; (25 pounds) (3600 calories per pound).
Break even caloric input per day to lose weight = 1300 calories.
Planned caloric daily intake based on proposed method = 1000 calories.
90,000 calories/300 calories = 300 days = 43 weeks = 10 months

Figure 6.28

DO (implementing the plan)—The weight loss plan is put in place by Bart.

STUDY (checking the effectiveness of the plan)—An x-bar and R chart and their corresponding log sheet are made up to track Bart's daily morning weight. The subgroup on the control chart will be one week. When enough data is available, the x-bar and R chart, with their corresponding log sheets, will be analyzed to provide clues for Bart so that he can reduce variation in his weight and decrease his average weight to 145 pounds.

ACT (act)—The data collected on the x-bar and R charts will be used to modify the weight loss method, preparation of a weekly menu.

227

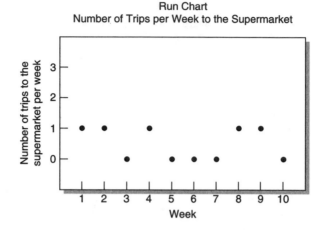

Figure 6.29

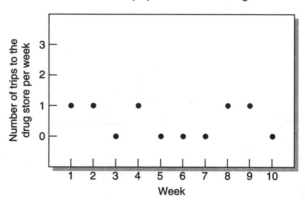

Figure 6.30

3. House Care Responsibilities:

PLAN (developing a plan)—An important process in Bart's life highlighted for attention is "sharing responsibility" with his spouse, especially household chores such as shopping at the supermarket, shopping

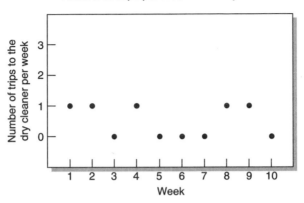

Run Chart
Number of Trips per Week to the Dry Cleaner

Figure 6.31

at the drug store, and picking up and dropping off clothes at the dry cleaner.

Bart collects data on each of these three activities (methods) for 10 weeks. The run charts are shown in Figures 6.29, 6.30, and 6.31.

Analysis of the run charts in Figures 6.29, 6.30, and 6.31 leads Bart to the realization that he needs to develop methods for "sharing responsibilities." He develops the flow charts (methods) shown in Figures 6.32, 6.33, and 6.34.

DO (implementing the plan)—Bart records the number of trips to each location per week after development of the methods. The data are shown in Figures 6.35, 6.36, and 6.37.

STUDY (checking the effectiveness of the plan)—The records show that all three targets are being met using the above methods.

Method for Shopping at Supermarket

Figure 6.32

230

Method for Shopping at Drug Store

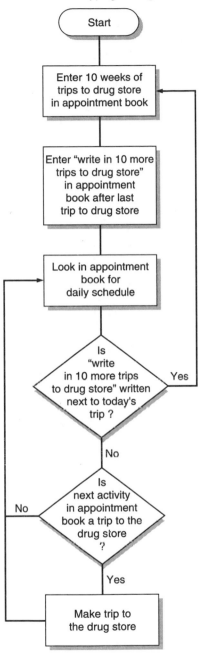

Figure 6.33

231

Method for Shopping at Dry Cleaner

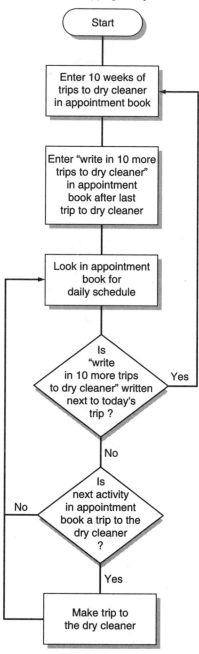

Figure 6.34

Personal Example of Policy Management

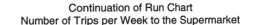

Continuation of Run Chart
Number of Trips per Week to the Supermarket

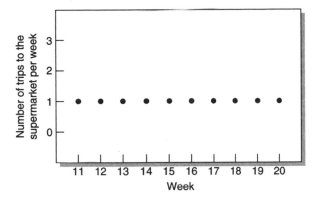

Figure 6.35

Continuation of Run Chart
Number of Trips per Week to the Drug Store

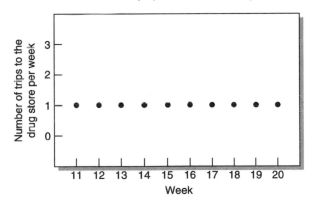

Figure 6.36

ACT (act)—Action to modify current methods is taken if a trend develops indicating failure of the methods to meet targets. Continuous monitoring and documentation of the causes for additional trips will help modify the current practices and assure achievement of targets.

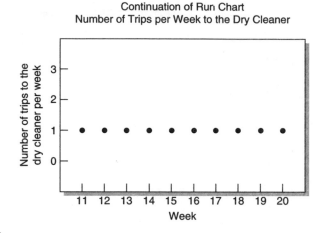

Figure 6.37

(3) Policy Implementation. All methods in the improvement plan are implemented and monitored on a weekly basis: exercise regimen, trips to the supermarket, trips to drug store, trips to dry cleaner, and dietary plan. (Note: the exercise regimen is discussed in Daily Management, Chapter 4). All methods are yielding predicted results (see Figures 6.38, 6.39, 6.40, and 6.41).

(4) Policy Study and Feedback. All methods implemented in the improvement plan are subject to monthly management reviews by Bart. He finds that methods are yielding predicted results. A year-end management review will be conducted at the appropriate time to determine if methods remain effective in respect to optimization of Bart's interdependent system of stakeholders.

Personal Example of Policy Management

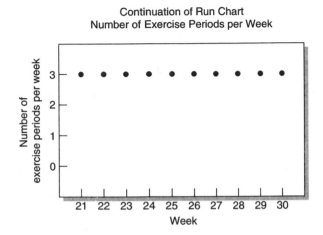

Continuation of Run Chart
Number of Exercise Periods per Week

Figure 6.38

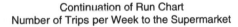
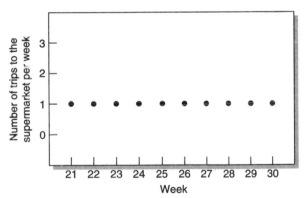

Continuation of Run Chart
Number of Trips per Week to the Supermarket

Figure 6.39

(5) Presidential Review. Presidential Review in the case study of personal policy management is equivalent to the yearly management reviews conducted by Bart of his strategic and improvement plans.

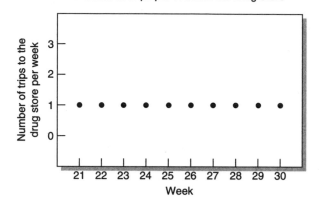

Figure 6.40

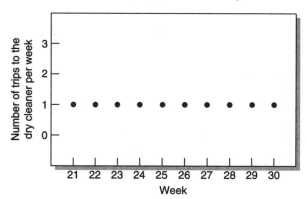

Figure 6.41

Summary

Chapter 6 discusses policy management, Prong Four of the quality management model presented in this book. Policy Management is performed by turning the PDSA

236

cycle to improve and innovate the methods responsible for the difference between corporate results and corporate targets, or to change the direction of an organization. Policy Management includes setting policy, deploying policy, studying policy, providing feedback to employees on policy, and conducting Presidential Reviews of policy. Policy Management is accomplished through the workings of an interlocking system of committees, including the Executive Committee (EC), the Policy Deployment Committee (PDC), Local Steering Teams (LSTs), and Project Teams.

The President conducts an initial Presidential Review to determine the state of the organization and to develop a plan of action for the promotion of corporate policy. This promotes a dialogue between the President and mid-level management and brings out information about problems. After a few rounds of Presidential Reviews, the President will have a good understanding of the major problems facing the organization and their possible causes.

The Executive Committee (EC) is responsible for setting the strategic plan for the entire organization. That includes establishing values and beliefs, developing statements of vision and mission, and preparing a draft set of strategic objectives. Techniques such as force field analysis, SWOT analysis, "Voice of the Customer," and "Voice of the Business" are used to

237

gather information and develop strategic objectives.

Members of the Policy Deployment Committee (PDC) develop a set of integrated improvement plans to promote the strategic objectives. The members of the PDC use tools such as gap analysis, Pareto diagrams, and cause-and-effect diagrams to develop the departmental and corporate improvement plans needed to promote departmental and corporate strategic objectives. The members of the Local Steering Teams (LSTs) are responsible for coordinating and carrying out the projects set up in the corporate and departmental improvement plans.

Strategic objectives and improvement plans are deployed by the PDC through assignment of responsibility for action to people or groups of people in departments. Techniques used in policy deployment include catchball and flag diagrams.

Policy is implemented when teams work on projects to improve and/or innovate processes. It is also implemented when departments use the revised processes and measure their results in respect to improvement plans and strategic objectives.

Periodic management reviews are conducted at two levels. First, the members of the EC review progress toward each strategic objective and its improvement plans monthly. Second, the members of the PDC and appropriate LSTs review progress for each project. The purpose of these reviews is to provide feedback to project team members that promotes process improvement efforts.

An application of policy management to a person's life is presented in this chapter. This example demonstrates all the steps of policy management and how to implement them.

Appendix 1

The Voice of the Customer

The term "customer" includes external customers and indirect customers.[9] External customers are the organizations or individuals who buy or use an organization's goods or services. Indirect customers are organizations which guard the welfare of external customers; for example, regulatory commissions and governmental agencies.

The "Voice of the Customer"[10] is a tool used to define the ever-changing market seg-

---

9. The term "indirect customers" was developed by Florida Power & Light Company. See FPL's Total Quality Management, Unit 12, page 11.
10. The authors believe that the term "Voice of the Customer" was developed by Florida Power & Light Company. Much of the information in this section was paraphrased from: FPL's Total Quality Management - Participant Handbook, 1st ed., Copyright ©1990 by the University of Miami Institute for the Study of Quality in Manufacturing and Service and QUALTEC, INC. (An FPL Subsidiary), see Unit 12, pp. 4 and 10-22.

ments for customers, determine and prioritize the customer requirements of each market segment, identify the processes (methods) used to respond to the customer requirements of each market segment, construct a matrix that explains the relationships between "the customer requirements of each market segment" and "the processes (methods) used to respond to the customer requirements," and prioritize the processes (methods) used to respond to customer requirements. Data collected from a "Voice of the Customer" analysis is used to formulate the strategic objectives of an organization. The steps for conducting a "Voice of the Customer" study are shown below.

(1) Define the ever-changing market segments for customers. The term "market segment" explains the dynamic and changing homogeneous groupings of customers in respect to the demographic, psychographic, and purchasing behavior variables that affect their decision to purchase and/or use a good or service. Focus groups, as well as other methods, are used to identify customer requirements for each market segment. Special care is taken to identify and define the customer requirements of noncustomers and future market segments.

(2) Determine and prioritize the customer requirements of each market segment. Management collects and analyzes observational, survey, and experimental data to understand the "Voice of the Customer" by

market segment. The question asked of a sample of customers from each market segment is, "From your perspective, what requirements must the organization surpass to pursue the mission statement?"

Prioritized List of Residential Customer's Requirements
Florida Power & Light Company

Direct Quality Requirements (What customers want)		Total Weight
1.	Quality Repair Work	9.42
2.	Accurate Electric Bills	9.41
3.	Honest Trustworthy Management	9.33
4.	Safely Maintained Company Equipment	9.27
5.	Fair Treatment of All Customers	9.27
6.	Friendly and Courteous Employees	9.26
7.	No Damage to Customers' or Public Property	9.17
8.	Accurate Answers to Questions	9.15
9.	Quickly Restored Power	9.14
10.	Safe Nuclear Plants	9.10
11.	Low Environmental Pollution	9.03
12.	Electricity-Good Value for the Money	9.01
13.	Timely Actions on Customers' Complaints/Concern for Customers' Problems	8.99

Figure A.1
Source: FPL TQM, Qualtec, Inc.,1990.

For example, Figure A.1[11] shows a prioritized list of customer requirements that were collected by randomly sampling Florida Power & Light residential customers. For each market segment, each customer requirement is scored on three scales: first, an importance to the customer scale; second, a

---

11. This figure is taken from *FPL's Total Quality Management,* Unit 12, page 13.

current level of performance in the eyes of the customer scale; and third, a desired level of performance by management to optimize the interdependent system of stakeholders scale. The "total weight" is computed for each customer requirement in each market segment. "Total weight" is a measure of the need to take action on a customer requirement.[12] See the right side of Figure A.1.

The "importance to the customer" scale quantifies the importance of customer requirements for each market segment. It does not quantify how well the organization is currently handling customer requirements or how much improvement is required in respect to customer requirements. The scale is a one (1) to five (5) scale: 1 = very unimportant and 5 = very important. "Importance to the customer" scores are obtained by computing the average ratings for each customer requirement for each market segment from survey and/or focus group data.

The "current level of performance" scale quantifies the gap between customer requirements and organizational performance. This scale is a one (1) to five (5) scale: 1 = very large gap and 5 = very small gap. The measure of current performance scale is obtained by computing the average ratings

12. This procedure for prioritizing customer requirements is adapted from the Quality Function Deployment methods of Dr. Akao.

from survey or focus group data for each customer requirement for each market segment from the following question: "How is the organization doing in respect to exceeding customer requirement x?" Customer requirements that show a "significant" gap are targeted for further study via gap analysis. For each customer requirement and market segment, gap analysis requires a measure of customer requirements (see "importance to the customer" scale) and a measure of current organizational performance (see "current level of importance" scale) to highlight the customer requirements that should be studied further with gap analysis. Gap analysis is a procedure for studying the root cause(s) of the difference between customer requirements and organizational performance. It is based on the analysis of relevant data. Many different tools are helpful in gap analysis; for example, flowcharting, the seven basic QC tools, and benchmarking. For example, the members of the EC might assign a group of staff personnel to study the root causes of the gap for a particular customer requirement for a particular market segment. The group might study the gap over time and determine that it is stable and contains only common variation. Next, they could construct a Pareto diagram of the common causes of the gap, isolate the most significant common cause, and develop a cause-and-effect diagram of its causes. Next, the staff personnel would study the correlation between the suspected root cause and the most significant cause of the gap. If the staff personnel found the correlation to be significant, they would recommend to the members of the EC a plan of action for improving the current level of performance for that customer requirement.

The "desired level of performance" scale quantifies the desired level of performance for each customer requirement, for each market segment. The scale is a one (1) to five (5) scale: 1 = small improvement in the organization's ability to exceed a customer requirement, and 5 = large improvement in the organization's ability to exceed a customer requirement. "Desired level of performance" scores are developed by staff personnel assigned by the EC. They conduct analyses of the levels of performance required for each customer requirement, for each market segment, to stay ahead of other organizations in the industry (using benchmarking) and future customer requirements.

The "total weight" score is a measure of the importance of the gap for each customer requirement, in each market segment. "Total weight" scores are computed using the following formula:

Total Weight = $[I \times D]/C$
   where:
   I = importance to the customer
   D = desired level of performance
   C = current level of performance

(3) Identify the processes (methods) used to respond to the needs and wants of each market segment and indirect customer. It is critical that the needs and wants of each appropriate market segment or indirect customer be serviced by identifiable methods. Customer needs and wants are translated into improved and innovated methods. This translation is accomplished by asking what methods are necessary to respond to each customer need or want. Figure A.2 may be helpful.[13]

Processes Necessary to Respond to Customer's
Requirements

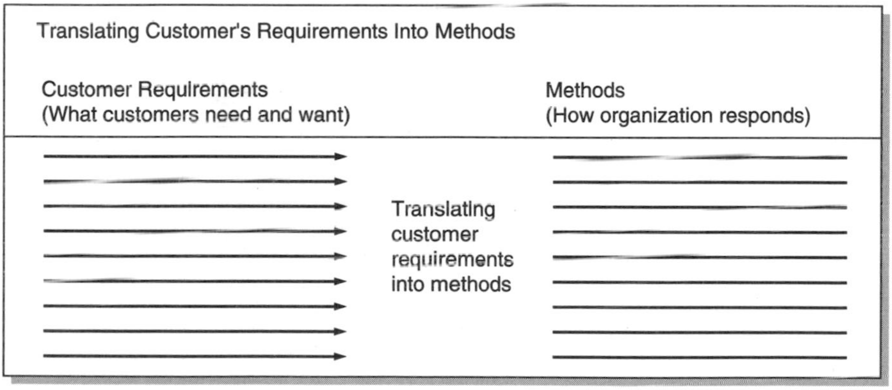

Figure A.2

(4) Construct a matrix that explains the relationships (cells of the matrix) between "customer requirements" (rows) and "the processes (methods) used to respond to customer requirements" (columns), for each

---

13. This chart is paraphrased from *FPL's Total Quality Management,* unit 12, page 15.

market segment and each indirect customer. All matrices should have the same columns.

The relationships shown in each cell of each matrix are determined by a group of staff personnel assigned this responsibility by the EC. The staff uses its knowledge of the organization and customers, along with that of other knowledgeable people, to determine the relationships. The staff members assigned to determine the relationships between the rows and columns keep a record of their logic for each symbol placed in the matrix, so they will not be second-guessed at a later date! Relationships are measured on the following scale: 3 = strong relationship, 2 = moderate relationship, 1 = weak relationship, and blank = no relationship. Sometimes, a doughnut symbol is used for a 3, a circle symbol is used for a 2, and a triangle symbol is used for a 1. The above numbers or symbols are used whether the relationships are positive or negative. A matrix showing the needs and wants of a particular market segment and the methods needed to respond to the needs and wants of the customers in the market segment can be seen in Figure A.3.

Every customer requirement must be adequately serviced by one or more methods. If a customer requirement is not being serviced by any method (or not adequately serviced), one or more methods are developed to service the customer requirement. If a method is not servicing (directly or in-

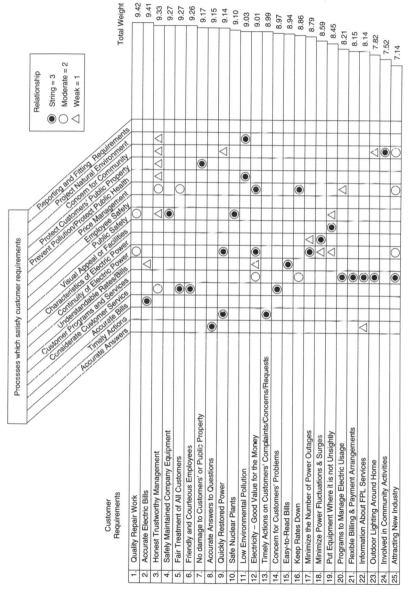

Figure A.3
Source: FPL TQM, Qualtec, Inc., 1990.

directly) at least one customer requirement, the method is dropped or receives decreased attention by stakeholders.

(5) Prioritize the processes (methods) used to respond to customer requirements for attention in the strategic objectives of the organization. Prioritization of methods is accomplished by the following procedure:

a. Compute the unnormalized weights (see Figure A.4) for each process, for a given market segment or indirect customer. For a given process (column in Figure A.3), multiply the "total weight" score for each customer requirement by the relationship score between that process and all customer requirements, and add all scores in a column. For example, the unnormalized weights for the process's "accurate answers" and "timely actions" are computed as follows::

Accurate answers:

$35.59 = (9.15\,[3] + 8.14\,[1])$, where

9.15 = the total weight for "accurate answers to questions,"

8.14 = the total weight for "information about FPL services,"

3 = the relationship between "accurate answers" and "accurate answers to question," and

1 = the relationship between "accurate answers" and "information about FPL services."

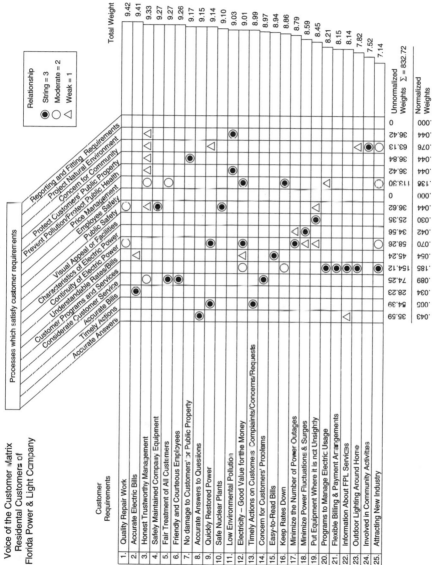

Figure A.4
Source: FPL TQM, Qualtec, Inc., 1990.

Timely answers:

54.39 = (9.14 [3] + 8.99 [3]). See Figure A.4.

b. Normalize the weighted values by dividing the individual weighted values by the sum of all weighted values (see Figure A.4).

c. Prioritize the normalized weighted values over all methods to provide input into the selection of strategic objectives for the organization. For example, the above analysis indicates that "timely answers" would receive a higher priority for attention than "accurate answers."

Appendix 2

Voice of the Business

The "Voice of the Business" is a tool for collecting and analyzing data about employee requirements (e.g., concerns and fears) in respect to the mission of an organization. "Voice of the Business" studies require that all groups of employees answer the following question: "What requirements (e.g., concerns and fears) do you have in respect to the organization pursuing its mission?" Data from the answer to this question helps to formulate the strategic objectives of an organization. The procedure for conducting a "Voice of the Business" study is described below.

(1) Collect and analyze the answers to the question posed above for each employee group, for example, top management, middle management, first line supervisors, and hourly employees. Brainstorming sessions,

focus groups, surveys, and management reviews are examples of tools that are useful in collecting information about the above question. Affinity diagrams, interrelationship diagraphs, and cause-and-effect diagrams are examples of tools that can be used to analyze the answers to the above question. These tools are discussed in Gitlow, H. and PMI, *Planning for Quality, Productivity and Competitive Position*, Dow Jones-Irwin (Homewood, IL), 1990.

(2) See step 2 in "Voice of the Customer." Determine and prioritize the employee requirements of each employee segment. Employee requirements are determined for each employee group, just as customer requirements are determined for each market segment and indirect customer.

(3) Identify the processes (methods) used to surpass the employee requirements for each employee group. These processes are the same as or additions to the processes used to address the customer requirements in a "Voice of the Customer" study. Employee requirements are used in developing strategic objectives for the organization

(4) Construct a matrix that explains the relationships (cells of the matrix) between "employee requirements" (rows) and "the processes (methods) used to respond to employee requirements" (columns), for each employee segment. All matrices should have the same columns. See step 4 in "Voice of the Customer."

(5) Prioritize the processes (methods) used to respond to employee requirements for attention in the strategic objectives of the organization. See step 5 in "Voice of the Customer."

Appendix 3

Table of Tables
Introduction

The original concept of the table of tables was developed by the members of the Research, Economics, and Forecasting Department of Florida Power & Light Company. The Table of Tables presented here is a variant of the Florida Power & Light Table of Tables. It considers customer requirements and employee requirements. The table of tables creates one prioritized list of processes (methods) to be highlighted for attention in the strategic objectives of the organization.

Building a Table of Tables[14]

A graphic mock-up of a Tables of Tables can be seen in Figure B.1.

Please note that all the "Voice of the Customer" subtables on the left side of the table of tables (there are three) and the "Voice of the Business" subtables shown on the right side of the table of tables (there are five) share a common set of processes (methods) in their columns. The "Voice of the Customer" and "Voice of the Business" studies all

---

14. Paraphrased from Research, Economics, and Forecasting Department, *Supplement to the Customer Needs Table of Tables,*" version 5, Florida Power & Light Company, 1990, p.3.

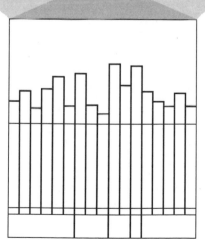

Figure B.1
Source: Florida Power & Light Company

result in prioritized lists of the common set of processes (methods). The table of tables globally prioritizes the common processes from each sub table.

The group of staff employees selected by the EC establishes a weight for the process priorities from each direct and indirect customer group (subtable) in the "Voice of the Customer" analysis and a similar weight for each employee group in the "Voice of the Business" analysis. For example, each of the three customer groups on the left side of Figure B.1 could receive equal weights of 0.333, 0.333, and 0.333, while the five employee groups on the right side of Figure B.1 could receive weights determined by the members of the EC, which are based on their assessment of the impact of each employee group on the organization. For example, employee group 1 may receive 0.10, employee group 2 may receive 0.50, employee group 3 may receive 0.05, employee group 4 may receive 0.05, and employee group 5 may receive 0.30.

The normalized scores in each subtable are multiplied by the appropriate subtable weight. The weighted normalized scores are summed over all tables for the left and right sides of the table of tables.

The members of EC weight the relative impact of the "Voice of the Customer" and the "Voice of the Business" on the organization. For example, the "Voice of the Customer" weighted normalized scores may receive a

Customer Needs Table of Tables
DIRECT NEEDS

Quality Requirements

Quality Elements

Quality Elements (column headers, left to right):

1. Accurate Answers/Timely Actions
2. Accurate Bills
3. Considerate Customer Service
4. Energy Management Assistance
5. Continuity of Service
6. Understandable Rates/Bills
7. Character of Service
8. Capacity
9. Public Safety
10. Prevent Pollution/Protect Public Health
11. Employee Safety
12. Price
13. Rate Options
14. Financial Integrity
15. Protect Property & Equipment
16. Concern for Community
17. Visual Appeal
18. Protect Natural Environment
19. Reporting & Filing Requirements

Residential

#	Quality Requirement	Importance of Requirements
1.	QUALITY REPAIRS	9.66
2.	HONEST TRUSTWORTHY MANAGEMENT	9.58
3.	ACCURATE ELECTRIC BILLS	9.57
4.	SAFELY MAINTAIN EQUIPMENT	9.57
5.	FAIR TREATMENT OF CUSTOMERS	9.52
6.	RESTORE POWER QUICKLY	9.50
7.	SAFE NUCLEAR PLANTS	9.50
8.	ACCURATE ANSWERS TO QUESTIONS	9.48
9.	ELECTRICITY – GOOD VALUE FOR THE MONEY	9.47
10.	FRIENDLY COURTEOUS EMPLOYEES	9.46
11.	KEEP RATES FROM GOING UP	9.43
12.	NOT DAMAGING PROPERTY	9.41
13.	LITTLE ENVIRONMENT POLLUTION	9.41
14.	CONCERN FOR CUSTOMERS' PROBLEMS	9.31
15.	TIMELY ACTIONS ON CUSTOMERS' COMPLAINTS	9.31
16.	MINIMIZE THE NUMBER OF POWER OUTAGES	9.15
17.	EASY-TO-READ BILLS	8.94
18.	PUT EQUIPMENT WHERE IT IS NOT UNSIGHTLY	8.73
19.	PROGRAMS TO MANAGE ELECTRIC USAGE	8.59
20.	PAYMENT ARRANGEMENTS – PAST DUE BILLS	8.14
21.	INVOLVED IN COMMUNITY ACTIVITIES	7.05

Sale For Resale

#	Quality Requirement
1.	ACCURATE ELECTRIC BILL
2.	ACCURATE ANSWERS TO QUESTIONS
3.	RESTORING POWER QUICKLY
4.	MINIMIZING POWER OUTAGES
5.	MEET CONTRACT DEMANDS
6.	QUALITY REPAIRS
7.	FAIR TREATMENT
8.	TIMELY ACTIONS
9.	UNDERSTANDABLE RATES
10.	CONCERN FOR CUSTOMERS
11.	PERMANENTLY ASSIGN CUSTOMER REP.
12.	FORECAST OF FUTURE ELECTRICITY CHARGES
13.	OFFER RATE OPTIONS

Column total values (bottom of chart, left to right): 3.43, 5.00, 1.13, 1.72, 3.18, 1.96, 0.59, 0.47, 3.88, 1.48, 0.00, 3.01, 0.00, 1.18, 1.00, 2.13, 0.60, 0.00

LEGEND
Relationship
- ● Strong
- ○ Moderate
- △ Weak

Figure B.2 *(Page 1 of 3)*
See Overall Ranking of Corporate Quality Elements on page 257.

Customer Needs Table of Tables

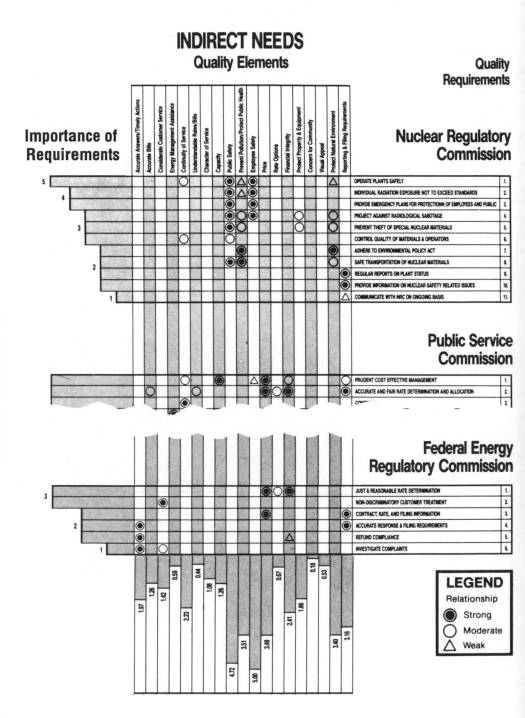

Figure B.2 *(Page 2 of 3)*
See Overall Ranking of Corporate Quality Elements on page 257.

Customer Needs Table of Tables

Weighting of Direct Needs

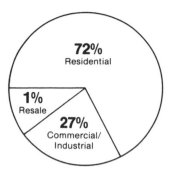

- **72%** Residential
- **1%** Resale
- **27%** Commercial/Industrial

Weighting of Indirect Needs

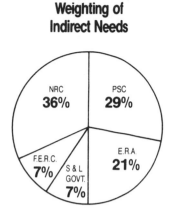

- NRC **36%**
- PSC **29%**
- F.E.R.C. **7%**
- S & L GOVT. **7%**
- E.R.A. **21%**

NOTES
*Importance of Requirements

1. Residential and C/I: Mean rating (scale of 1-10) of customers responding to Satisfaction Survey.

2. Resale: 1-3 rating based on judgement of staff representing customer segment.

3. NRC, ERA: 1-5 scale based on consequence of violation.

4. Gov't, PSC, and FERC: 1-3 scale based on consequence of violation.

The Table of Tables represents FPL's customers' needs and their importance ratings of these needs. It does not represent the company's ranking of functional areas.

©Copyright 1988 Florida Power & Light Company

Overall Ranking of Corporate Quality Elements

Category	Element	Value
SALES AND SERVICE QUALITY	Accurate Answers/Timely Actions	5.39
	Accurate Bills	2.39
	Considerate Customer Service	6.42
	Energy Management Assistance	2.31
	Continuity of Service	5.42
	Understandable Rates/Bills	2.40
DELIVERY	Character of Service	1.73
	Capacity	1.68
SAFETY	Public Safety	8.59
	Prevent Pollution/Protect Public Health	4.99
	Employee Safety	5.00
COST	Price	6.50
	Rate Options	1.85
	Financial Integrity	2.41
CORPORATE RESPONSIBILITY	Protect Property & Equipment	3.26
	Concern for Community	2.31
	Visual Appeal	1.53
	Protect Natural Environment	4.49
	Reporting & Filing Requirements	3.16

Figure B.2 *(Page 3 of 3)*

relative importance of 0.75, while the "Voice of the Business" normalized scores receive a relative importance of 0.25.

Finally, the weighted normalized scores for the "Voice of the Customer" and the "Voice of the Business" are multiplied by the relative weights of each voice. This results in one prioritized list of processes (methods) to be used as input in the selection of strategic objectives for the organization.

Case Study

The Table of Tables developed by Florida Power & Light Company in 1988 to input the "Voice of the Customer" data into their policy management process is shown in Figure B.2. Figure B.2 demonstrates how FP&L defined "direct needs" as being the desires of their three market segments for external customers (residential, industrial, sale for resale), only residential and sale for resale shown. Figure B.2 also shows how FP&L defined "indirect needs" as being the concerns of their regulators and government agencies (NRC, PSC, ERA, State and Local governments, and the FERC), only NRC, PSC, and FERC shown. The Table of Tables demonstrates how FP&L prioritized its quality elements (what it does) to better satisfy customer needs and wants via policy management.

Index

INDEX

INDEX

I NDEX

Detailed Fork Model
for Quality Management

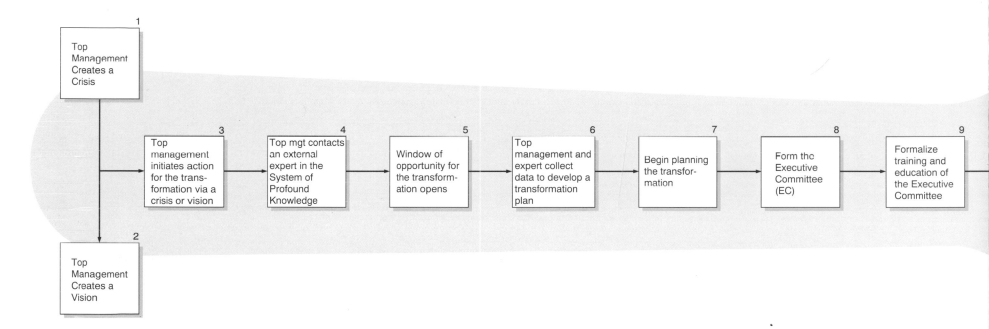

1 Top Management Creates a Crisis

2 Top Management Creates a Vision

3 Top management initiates action for the transformation via a crisis or vision

4 Top mgt contacts an external expert in the System of Profound Knowledge

5 Window of opportunity for the transformation opens

6 Top management and expert collect data to develop a transformation plan

7 Begin planning the transformation

8 Form the Executive Committee (EC)

9 Formalize training and education of the Executive Committee

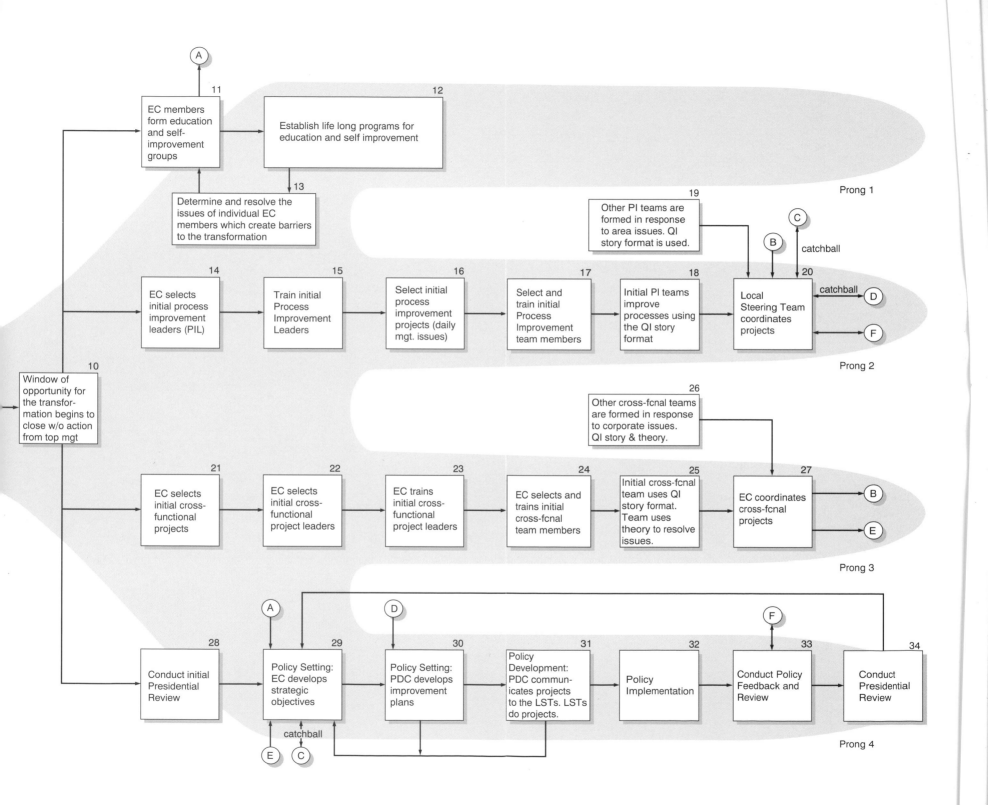

Prong 1

(A)

11 — EC members form education and self-improvement groups

12 — Establish life long programs for education and self improvement

13 — Determine and resolve the issues of individual EC members which create barriers to the transformation

Prong 2

19 — Other PI teams are formed in response to area issues. QI story format is used.

(C) catchball

(B)

14 — EC selects initial process improvement leaders (PIL)

15 — Train initial Process Improvement Leaders

16 — Select initial process improvement projects (daily mgt. issues)

17 — Select and train initial Process Improvement team members

18 — Initial PI teams improve processes using the QI story format

20 — Local Steering Team coordinates projects

catchball (D)

(F)

10 — Window of opportunity for the transformation begins to close w/o action from top mgt

Prong 3

26 — Other cross-fcnal teams are formed in response to corporate issues. QI story & theory.

21 — EC selects initial cross-functional projects

22 — EC selects initial cross-functional project leaders

23 — EC trains initial cross-functional project leaders

24 — EC selects and trains initial cross-fcnal team members

25 — Initial cross-fcnal team uses QI story format. Team uses theory to resolve issues.

27 — EC coordinates cross-fcnal projects

(B)

(E)

Prong 4

(A) (D) (F)

28 — Conduct initial Presidential Review

29 — Policy Setting: EC develops strategic objectives

30 — Policy Setting: PDC develops improvement plans

31 — Policy Development: PDC communicates projects to the LSTs. LSTs do projects.

32 — Policy Implementation

33 — Conduct Policy Feedback and Review

34 — Conduct Presidential Review

catchball

(E) (C)